THE PRACTICAL PREPPERS COMPLETE GUIDE TO DISASTER PREPAREDNESS

THE
PRACTICAL PREPPERS
COMPLETE GUIDE TO
DISASTER
PREPAREDNESS

Scott Hunt

THOMAS DUNNE BOOKS
ST. MARTIN'S GRIFFIN 〰 NEW YORK

The information available in and through this book is for general informational purposes only and is not intended to substitute for medical, legal, or other professional advice. The author and publisher do not accept responsibility for any adverse effects individuals may claim to experience, whether directly or indirectly, from the information contained in, or available through, this book.

THOMAS DUNNE BOOKS.
An imprint of St. Martin's Press.

THE PRACTICAL PREPPERS COMPLETE GUIDE TO DISASTER PREPAREDNESS. Copyright © 2014 by Practical Preppers LLC. All rights reserved. Printed in the United States of America. For information, address St. Martin's Press, 175 Fifth Avenue, New York, N.Y. 10010.

www.thomasdunnebooks.com
www.stmartins.com

Designed by Richard Oriolo

Library of Congress Cataloging-in-Publication Data
is available upon request.

ISBN 978-1-250-05564-4 (trade paperback)
ISBN 978-1-4668-5924-1 (e-book)

St. Martin's Griffin books may be purchased for educational, business, or promotional use. For information on bulk purchases, please contact Macmillan Corporate and Premium Sales Department at 1-800-221-7945, extension 5442, or write specialmarkets@macmillan.com.

10 9 8 7 6 5 4

To all those who look ahead, see what's coming, and prepare the best they can to help others. And, to those who when disaster strikes, head to the crisis to ease pain and suffering.

CONTENTS

ACKNOWLEDGMENTS

I would like to acknowledge Jesus, my Lord and Savior, who has gone to prepare a place for me.

This book would not have been possible without the support and encouragement of my lovely wife, Lori. Her desire to be prepared and her medical expertise were invaluable to the writing of the book.

A special thanks to my sweet children, Reba, Ellie, Sara, and Elijah, who helped out so much around the house and farm so I could have more time to devote to the book.

Josh Hudson for sweating the details of finding and photographing the images for the book.

Anne Brewer of St. Martin's Press for her foresight and assistance throughout the project.

INTRODUCTION

What are you preparing for? The basic necessities to survive any disaster scenario are usually all the same. This is one of the reasons I chose to write this book. Focusing too narrowly on just one doomsday concern can lead to the neglect of general life-saving solutions that will be useful no matter the situation. Three of the primary lessons you will discover as you read through the following chapters revolve around the importance of assessing your current situation, building upon or refining existing preps, and the difference between sustainable and grid-dependent systems integral to your survival.

As I was writing chapter 1 of this book, the most powerful storm on record was occurring. Super Typhoon Haiyan was the most powerful recorded typhoon to ever hit land and likely the deadliest natural disaster to hit the Philippines. During the storm I was contacted by a prepper and YouTube subscriber from the Philippines who, because of his preparations, had food and water. The world we live in is very unstable. We are seeing natural disasters of biblical proportions. In Sumatra in 2004 at least 280,000 people were killed by a tsunami. The Fukushima disaster in 2011 is a prime example of the deadly nature of man-made accidents. Who would have ever thought a tsunami, earthquake, and nuclear disaster could happen all at once? In the United States, Katrina in 2005 was the "perfect storm." New Orleans is a city built eight feet below sea level, with aging infrastructure and poor municipal planning. NOLA residents were lured into a false sense of security; after all, the Crescent City had weathered a multitude of hurricanes before. Hurricane Sandy in 2012 was a new hybrid storm—a blizzard/hurricane never before recorded—a "Superstorm." In 2013, Colorado suffered massive wildfires and flooding while South Dakota experienced an early season blizzard that killed seventy-five thousand cows. The hits just keep on coming.

The federal government's continued lack of action in regard to the nation's most often ignored piece of infrastructure, the power grid, could pose a disastrous future for America. The power grid is incredibly fragile, and most people who are preparing for TEOTWAWKI (The End Of The World As We Know It) expect that a disaster will bring it down. Preparing for disruption of services is a noble venture that gives peace of mind. Whether it is an economic downturn or a disruption from a solar flare that destroys life as we know it, the preparedness techniques are all the same. Our long-distance systems, like widely distributed power, medicine, and food, make us extremely susceptible to enemies or weather events. Living sustainably offers an independent existence.

Planning is the key to Preparedness. This book details straightforward solutions that must be implemented before the disaster occurs. Each chapter is structured in a way that begins with simple methods and then progresses to more complex strategies. Each chapter starts out with concepts and ideas that apply to the urban as well as the rural prepper. We believe you should be prepared no matter where you live. In order to alleviate suffering, help your unprepared neighbors, and curtail civil unrest, you must at least consider implementing what you will learn in this book. Everything Practical Preppers will share with you will be ideas that can be used in everyday life and not just for "rainy day" events.

ABOUT THE AUTHOR

There is no one event I can call a "watershed moment" where I became passionate about self-sufficiency and being prepared for adverse events. I am very thankful for all God has allowed me to be exposed to: the good, the bad, and the ugly. I was exposed to how things work in my life in my dad's body shop, on my uncle's dairy and vegetable farm, in my grandparents' businesses in the George Rickey fabrication workshop, in my stepfather's logging operation, and in serving three years with the U.S. Naval Sea Cadets through another uncle. I had a terrific opportunity to be educated at an esteemed engineering institution, RPI (Rensselaer Polytechnic Institute). A decade at Michelin Tire Corporation afforded me opportunities to apply my engineering education and turn it to skill. What brought balance to my life was becoming a Christian (spiritual preparedness), and being a pastor for a decade allowed me to see plenty of human suffering—foreign and domestic.

I had the privilege to be cast on the pilot episode of *Doomsday Preppers* in 2011. The series became the most watched in Nat Geo TV history. After the pilot and before the series began, we were contracted with the production company to perform all assessments and evaluations of each prepper casted. At the time of writing, we have completed three seasons. We were also featured on Nat Geo's webisodes teaching people how to obtain necessary preparations before a disaster occurs. During the filming we were consulted on various scenarios and provided technical support to the production staff. I also designed and installed an off-grid water system for the family featured on *Doomsday Castle*.

When it comes to preparedness, it boils down to storage and networking. Storing water, food, energy, medical supplies, ammunition, tools, and fuel is a must. Establishing a network of people you can communicate with, learn from, and possibly live with will greatly increase your level of preparedness. "Making hay while the sun shines" is how I live my life. It not only allows me to weather the fluctuations in my own life, but also the disasters. I want to eliminate the image of preppers having an attitude of "I live and you die." Being prepared for adversity gives opportunity to help those who are overwhelmed. A shepherd takes care of the sheep, and an engineer implements solutions to do just that.

When people wake up to the potential threats in the world around them they become overwhelmed. Preparedness empowers individuals, removes fear, and reduces anxiety. I have seen the mistakes of out-of-balance preparedness and its waste of precious resources. I hope this book will save you money and time. As you go through this book, take an inventory of your weaknesses and begin to address them. We have found that sustainable solutions not only offer a peace of mind but a rewarding life-style. I want you to be empowered to begin your journey in preparedness so you can prepare—to live.

WATER
Keep Your Head Above Water!

We never know the worth of water till the well is dry.

—Thomas Fuller

Will you have enough water when a crisis occurs? The average American consumes approximately 1,600 gallons each day. Stop doing the math in your head. Yes, a human being would likely drown if they actually drank that much water in a single twenty-four-hour period. By consume, I mean use—the truest form of the definition of consumption.

Ponder for just a moment how often you turn on the faucet, relax in a hot shower, or push down a toilet handle each day. These few simple examples are obviously among the most important mundane water uses we must consider when attempting to grasp how much a single person depletes local water resources each day.

But if you start thinking larger, you'll see that a drop of water that fell on a wheat field this afternoon is going to be part of my sandwich bread five months from now. If it's a ham sandwich, a lot more water was used. It takes roughly 52 gallons of water to make one glass of milk. It takes more than 600 gallons to make a quarter-pound hamburger. A total of 2,800 gallons of water is used to make one pair of jeans.

Our daily lives carry a giant water footprint. Water is necessary for life. The sophistication of the society that an individual dwells in is determined by the amount of water consumed. While living in a first world country may be luxurious at the moment, such a scenario is not sustainable for long periods of time during either a man-made or natural disaster. The ability to support large groups of people living in high-population-density areas is greatly diminished during disasters.

Think about your water supply being cut off or contaminated. Who will survive? Those with clean, potable water will still be among the living after the dust clears. The human body can last for three to five days, at the most, without water. Securing a clean water source must be your primary preparedness objective, regardless what type of doomsday disaster you feel is looming on the horizon. When a catastrophe becomes reality, potable water will be in both high demand and short supply.

Once the reality of exactly how much water is typically consumed by your family each day sinks in, it is time to begin figuring out how to source clean water. In a first world country, municipal systems deliver clean water to residences by a vast array of pumps, pipes, filters, and chemicals that render open-water sources drinkable. These expensive systems serve the masses and usually provide seamless delivery of life-sustaining water. Individuals dwelling in population-dense areas can certainly store this water in appropriately sized containers.

Municipal water is typically treated with chemicals such as chlorine, fluoride, aluminum, and ammonia. Ammonia has had to be added in recent years. It combines with chlorine to form chloramines, which are now found in 20 percent of American water supplies. Water quality continues to deteriorate to the point where waste water treatment plants produce water that is more pure than the water produced by municipal water plants. The greatest challenge to the waste-water industry is the psychological barrier to the end product of waste-water treatment plants. The removal of unwanted contents will be dealt with in the purification section of this chapter. If you only have municipal water as your source, your *only* solution is to store enough for you to weather the storm. I am not belittling this solution—it is a great solution.

A trip to a third world country will really make you grateful for the municipal water systems we have in this country. On a trip to Nicaragua to drill wells, I learned that when the water is flowing from the tap you had better capture and store some of it. You could be taking a quick shower and the water just stops. When I first went in for a shower, I was wondering what the bucket was for in the shower. I did not make that mistake again and made sure, if there was water, that I filled the bucket first. It made me wonder how the source of that water was being treated, if at all, and with what chemicals. I now make a conscious effort to have a good water filter such as a Sawyer Mini with me when I travel.

Our overall objective for a disaster water plan is:

- Storage
- Resupply
- Purification

Let's examine storage first.

STORAGE

Water can be stored in a variety of containers and places. A few examples of containers include: 2-liter recycled soda bottles, 55-gallon plastic barrels, polyethylene doorway containers, bathtub water storage system, stackable BPA-free water containers, and large above- and underground cisterns. BPA is an industrial chemical found in plastics and has been linked to health concerns in children. Where you store water is very important as well. The best places to store are either underground or in a cool, dry place. How long you are storing water is greatly determined by the source you start with. Municipal water can be stored for long periods of time without further treatment.

We recommend treating all other sources of water with the methods found in the purification section of this chapter. If you store water in your home or apartment, remember water is very heavy, 8.35 pounds per gallon, so the flooring must be able to support the extra weight. Like many items stored, water must be rotated to stay fresh. Water that is stored too long runs the risk of algae growth and excessive bacterial growth. During a disaster there are so many contaminants that enter the public water supply, it is better to have water stored that you know is potable than to second-guess what is in the water.

Water Storage for the Urban Dweller

Storage options for the city resident include:

- **Fill recycled bottles or other sturdy containers from the tap and store in closets, on shelves, and under sinks and beds**
- **"WaterBrick International" products make water storage easy**
- **"WaterBOBs" for the bathtubs**

There are a lot of petrochemicals and heavy metals that end up in water sources during flooding, so we greatly encourage stored water at all times. For an urban prepper, water storage is of utmost importance because the ability to find and secure potable water during a disaster is limited. Store as much as you can. There are many approaches to storing water so choose at least one. I recommend Water Brick International products for apartment dwellers who are concerned about saving space. The stackable bricks are a great option for storing a lot of water yet not overcrowding the space—and can even be used as furniture! The bricks can be frozen and also placed in a refrigerator to help preserve perishable food when the power goes out. "WaterBObs" are plastic containers designed to fit most bathtubs and are an inexpensive way to store extra potable water. This is a great way to store water temporarily, such as when you know a heavy storm is coming.

How much water should you store? This all depends on the duration of the disaster, how many people must be covered, and what level of energy you are expending. Our rule of thumb is to store 1 to 2 gallons of potable water per day per person for a three-month period of time. That is 1,260 gallons for our family of six people! That is a lot of water but can easily be handled with one polyethylene cistern.

RESUPPLY: SOURCES AND DELIVERY

Once you do the math, it's not hard to see that it will be difficult to store enough water for your family's needs for more than a few weeks. Seeking out water sources and methods of delivery to your shelter can provide peace of mind when you contemplate a disaster that would cause interruption of normal services for more than a week.

Finding Water Sources on Your Property

If you live in a suburban or rural area, you may be able to tap into an existing water source on your property. When I am at an on-site consultation, I often refer to my dad telling me "If you ever buy a property that does not have a good water source, I will disown you." Many times when walking a site looking for water sources, people believe they have a reliable source, but in many cases the source is seasonal runoff that is easily contaminated. When I am walking a piece of land, I am looking for the largest trees, and certain flora—holly, ferns, poplar—knowing that they are tapped into life-sustaining water. Think of towns with names such as "Holly Springs" and "Poplar Springs"—communities that were settled around areas of reliable, plentiful water sources.

Another method without any scientific evidence to back it up is water dousing. One of the games I used to play as a child was to try to find the buried ax head or metal object that my grandfather buried in the garden. Using coat hangers, a forked branch from a green ironwood or willow branch, or welding rods, we scanned the ground until either the forked branch dove toward the ground or the metal rods made an X and we

DOUSING FOR WATER

started to dig. To prove we weren't cheating we were blindfolded. First one to find the ax head wins! I still use dousing to find buried water lines and power lines before I dig on my property, but it is not a method I would bet my life on when I am consulting at a client's location.

My big goal in this discussion on sources is for the individual to have control over their water during a disaster. You can hire a hydrogeologist, who can determine the best place on your property to locate a well. I did this to learn what they look for and why, so that when I consult with people on their water sources I can make sure I have covered every possible solution. Let's investigate the variety of water sources available and the concerns about the quality of these sources.

Wells

Wells are a great decentralized source of water and typically provide the safest long-term source of water for your shelter. There are many different types of wells. Generally they are drilled deep into bedrock or aquifers and

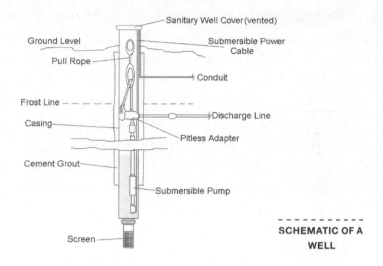

Sanitary Well Cover (vented)

Ground Level

Submersible Power
Cable

Pull Rope

Conduit

Frost Line

Discharge Line

Casing

Pitless Adapter

Cement Grout

Submersible Pump

Screen

**SCHEMATIC OF A
WELL**

are cased in steel or plastic to a depth ensuring protection from ground-water. *Groundwater* is the term generally describing water that has seeped from the surface into the soil. Groundwater can be easily contaminated with various chemicals, petroleum products, and other industrial runoff.

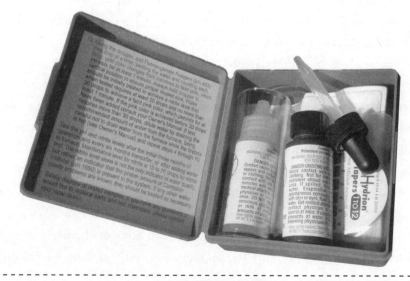

WATER-TESTING KIT

Proper well construction and bentonite grout prevent this groundwater from reaching the well water.

Because well water is not treated, special care is needed when storing it for long periods of time. The good news is that water is continually replaced in the well so it stays fresh. All natural water sources, like well water, contain coliform bacteria. The presence of coliform bacteria can indicate the presence of more dangerous bacteria, such as E. coli. At Practical Preppers, we recommend testing well water annually. If you are storing water for long periods of time, consider treating with any method listed in the purification section.

Types of Wells

- Hand-dug
- Bored
- Commercially drilled
- Artesian
- Jetted

If you can afford it and it is allowed in your area, we recommend commercially drilled deep wells. These wells are the ones that reach deep into the aquifers and safer water supplies. Depending on where you live, the shallower hand-dug and bored wells can provide a wonderful source of water, but are susceptible to drought and ground-water contamination. Many states have discontinued shallow well construction techniques and settled on commercially drilled deep wells. A bored well is large in diameter—two to three feet—and is therefore a safety concern. Children and pets have fallen into these wells, whereas they cannot in a commercial well, where the diameter is two to eight inches. If you have one of these types of wells we do not recommend abandoning it, for it provides a great off-grid supply of water. You should fit it with a larger diameter casing, which will prevent accidents and allow you to use a variety of pumping solutions. Well drilling typically requires a license but there are a few places where drilling your own well is legal. In South Carolina, for instance, a well can be hand drilled by the home owner as long as it meets the Department of Health and Environmental Control's (DHEC) specifications. The home owner must get a permit from DHEC before installing the well. We have used WaterStep hand drills for our hand-dug wells. Check your local statutes before beginning construction of a well.

Springs

Springs are literally fountains of clean water bubbling up to the surface of the soil. These usually occur in hilly terrain where fractures in the bedrock under the soil act as channels for underground water to travel upward. Gravity-fed springwater has been used for thousands of years as a way to sustain life. Communities naturally developed around springs in the founding of this country—Colorado Springs is a prime example. Little

SPRING BOX

COLLECTION SYSTEM

to no work is required to get the water out of the ground. Springs were used prior to refrigeration for storing food.

Like wells, they can contain coliform bacteria and they are susceptible to contamination from runoff. One of my favorite parts of a client's evaluation is walking their property and locating these water sources. Over a period of time, springs sediment in. They get hidden and can go underground. With a shovel I can probe into the ground to find the source, the springhead. Many springs have been ruined by bringing in heavy equipment because the water will take the path of least resistance. I want to give the water a path that is easily collected, filtered, and delivered to the end user.

Spring development has taken many forms over the years. Historically, spring development was done with one large springhouse built over the springhead. A springhead is the site where water flows to the ground surface. The springhouse is built over the springhead to keep animals and insects out. However, it can be hard to keep the springhead free of contamination and infiltration. We have found that capturing the spring with the smallest footprint at the springhead and providing for runoff protection greatly improves water quality. This water is then delivered to a smaller spring box that is easily maintained. From the spring box the water can be either pumped to higher elevations or delivered by gravity to a cistern and then to your shelter. If you are fortunate enough to have a naturally occurring spring on your property, we highly recommend you develop it. I have pumped water from my spring for seventeen years and it has supplied all our watering needs when it comes to gardening, raising livestock, and firefighting.

Rainwater

Rainwater is a significant and often overlooked source of water. A simple system of gutters and first-flush diverters on a roofline can collect large amounts of water, and cisterns placed below can store it until needed. There are many water-impoverished countries where this is a common

WATER STORAGE TANK

solution for water needs. The American Rainwater Catchment Systems Association is a great resource for DIYers. Americans do need to be aware of local laws, as this type of collection is not legal in certain parts of the United States.

Utilizing rainwater as a water source introduces contaminants not found in other water sources. Bird and bat fecal material, tree debris, industrial fallout, and building material contamination are among the common health concerns. Typical rainwater storage systems range from 55-gallon drums placed aboveground in series, to large underground concrete cisterns.

Open Sources

Open sources of water include lakes, ponds, and streams. This group requires filtration and/or chemical treatment as these are "living" sources, where wildlife congregate and derive their water. Humans are not generally able to tolerate the vast amount of bacteria, cysts, and viruses that are present in open-water sources. Waterborne diseases such as cholera, shigella, campylobacter, and giardia are just a few types of bacteria often present in open-water sources. Waterborne diseases are responsible for 3.4 million deaths each year. A total of 780 million people lack access to clean water around the world. The term *water poverty* describes the multitudes of people who, although surrounded by water, have nothing clean to drink. For these individuals, a large part of their lives is spent in securing biomass to burn to boil water.

The final open source of water is the ocean. Approximately 140 million square miles (362 million square kilometers) of the earth is encompassed by ocean. In contrast, the land surface is 58 million square miles (150 million square kilometers). Unfortunately for humans, there is 4 percent salinity in ocean water. Human bodies are only 0.9 percent salinity. When humans are forced to consume ocean water, the increase in salt intake causes more, not less, thirst. The drinking of ocean water will ultimately lead to death, as the salt cannot be excreted out fast enough by the kidneys. Currently there are two technologies that can render ocean water potable, reverse osmosis and distillation. Both will be discussed later in this chapter.

DELIVERY

The delivery of clean water to the user is always a topic of considerable interest to me. Since many people are preparing for disruptions in the usual delivery of water to the masses, Practical Preppers has many solutions at various costs. Obviously, some of these solutions are dependent on which source is being developed, the water requirements of the client, and the energy available.

Well Water Delivery

First we will examine well water delivery systems. Wells are drilled and capped by the well driller. In order to extract the water out of the ground, you must have a pump. Pumps use a variety of energy inputs ranging

SUCTION PUMP

from electrical to manual. Typical well pumps are dependent on grid or generator power. We will share some alternatives that will provide comparable amounts of water and pressures. Let's start off with simple manual pumps.

Types of Manual Pumps

- Suction pumps
- Lift pumps
- Force pumps

The static water level in a well is the important determinant of what type of hand pump can be used. The static water level refers to the distance

LIFT PUMP

from the surface to the top of the water in the well casing. It is physically impossible to suction lift water more than thirty-three feet. A suction pump works very similarly to how you use a straw to drink water. When you use a straw you create a vacuum on the inside of the straw. The pressure on the outside of the straw is greater, forcing the water to move up the straw. The maximum pressure you can produce is atmospheric pressure at sea level (14.7 psi). To convert pressure into elevation you multiply the pressure by 2.31 feet. At thirty-three feet, you can no longer create enough pressure to lift the water high enough to get it out of your well.

If your static level is higher in value than thirty-three feet, then you would have to use a lift or force pump. In reality, most suction-type hand pumps will not work on sources greater than twenty-five feet static. Also, as this is a physical law of fluids, the greater the elevation, the lower the static water level must be. The figure of thirty-three feet is a theoretical number, in reality it is a little less. In Denver, at an elevation of 5,280 feet, the pump can lift twenty-eight feet in theory. Suction hand pumps are of limited use in the United States as most wells are professionally drilled to great depths and have static water levels well beyond thirty-three feet. Also, they do not pump into pressurized systems, such as homes. Nonetheless, they are very reasonable in price, often below $50.

Lift pumps, such as Simple Pump, work by a completely different mechanism. They lift from a cylinder placed directly in the well water. As the lever arm is lifted up, the rods and piston go down. A lower ball valve inside the cylinder, which seals under pressure, and an upper seal inside the piston lifts and allows water to flow. When the lever arm is pushed down, the rods and piston go up. A whole column of water is lifted up and at the same time water goes into the pump cylinder from the bottom, getting ready for the next cycle. A force pump is similar but the action is reversed. When the piston is pushed down the water is forced up through the pump.

These pumps can work to maximum lift of three hundred feet. In general, about five gallons per minute can be pumped manually. These pumps can be installed right alongside the existing electrical pump thus

SHALLOW WELL JET PUMP

CONVERTIBLE WELL PUMP

SUBMERSIBLE WELL PUMP

allowing water to be delivered into the home without it having to be hand carried.

When I am working on a client's system, I have to take into account another concept, the Total Dynamic Head [TDH]. This is the distance from static water level up to the surface plus the increase in elevation from the surface to the terminal location, either a cistern or bladder tank in the house. TDH is used to specify the right pump for the job. One thing that is often overlooked in determining TDH is the friction loss in the delivery pipes. Many a DIYer has had to redo their systems because they chose too small a pipe diameter, thus greatly increasing the friction in the system to the point where the pump they hoped to use would no longer work.

Types of Power-Driven Well Pumps

- Shallow jet
- Convertible
- Submersible

Let's talk about three types of what I would call "grid" pumps that use standard household electricity in order to pump water from a well. These pumps rely on electricity (which you must have a plan to generate during a power outage), but have the advantage of lower cost compared to their off-grid counterparts. Shallow well jet and convertible well jet pumps are *not* submersible and are usually placed inside a protected area outside a well. Deep well submersible pumps typically are submerged inside your well.

For well depths in the range from 0–25 feet all three types of pumps can be used. In the range from 25–90 feet the convertible and the submersible can be used, and for wells deeper than ninety feet only the submersible can be used. Other factors, like the size of the well casing and how much water is required, will be used to determine what size horsepower (HP) pump will be needed.

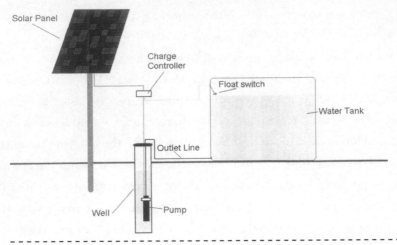

SOLAR WATER PUMPING SETUP

"PHASE TWO" SOLAR ARRAY

Types of Off-Grid Pumps

- Hydraulic ram pump
- Wind pump

Solar and Gravity

Depending on your well water depth there are several off-the-grid pumping solutions for delivering well water. One of the awesome things I have discovered is that these off-grid systems can, in most cases, be installed in parallel with your on-the-grid pump systems. This leads me to share with you my favorite off-grid well water pumping and delivery technique. I call these "Phase One" systems. If the location has the right lay of land—enough elevation and ground that is not ridiculously hard to install pipes in—I like to set cisterns at the top of the property and fill them via a solar water pumping station. This accomplishes several things. It eliminates the need for batteries that are usually the weakest link in most alternative energy systems. It also guarantees that you always have stored water, and it is much cheaper to store water than electricity. The water is then distributed to the home, the garden, the pond, and livestock via gravity. In many systems I install an overflow in the cistern that either returns the water to its source once the tank is full or delivers this excess water to a pond or garden. The side benefit of doing this is a cistern that is always fresh.

If there is not enough elevation on the property then we employ booster pumps that use solar to charge a small battery bank and thus provide power to the pump when it is needed. These are my "Phase Two" systems.

They provide volumes and pressures that match the on-grid systems but they use about 20 percent of the energy. It is very rewarding to be able to use a simple concept of water storage and delivery that uses either no grid power at all or a very small amount of power. To summarize and hopefully simplify my technique, I use the sun's energy to lift water and gravity to distribute. Storing the water allows me to "make hay" while the sun is shining.

Spring Water Delivery

If your water is sourced from a spring, and the water has been collected in a springbox, then any type of pump can be used to deliver the water

RIFE RAM PUMP

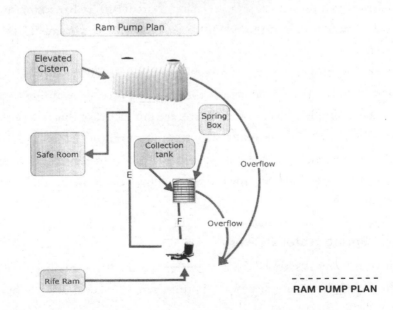

RAM PUMP PLAN

to its final destination. It is rare but some springs are located above the final destination and therefore gravity is all that is needed to deliver the water. Remember, when homesteads and farms were established before electricity they were located below these springs. Today folks go for the "view" but in the past they went for the water!

Hydraulic Rams

Sometimes, springheads will produce enough water that a hydraulic ram can be used to take that water and pump it up to an elevated cistern. These are awesome projects as the balancing of falling water, elevation, and ram pump size come into play. These pumps were one of the main distribution technologies before the advent of electricity. The first self-acting ram pump was invented by the Frenchman Joseph Michel Montgolfier (best known as a coinventor of the hot air balloon), in 1796 for raising water in his paper mill. By the end of the twentieth century interest in hydraulic rams has revived, due to the needs of sustainable technology in developing countries, and energy conservation in developed ones. In all of man's attempts at building a perpetual motion machine this is the closest I have seen in action. The deep *thump* of a ram is a mesmerizing sound if you ever have the privilege of walking up on one running. Many times, a spring will not produce enough water to actually run a ram pump but if there is a stream or pond nearby a carefully thought-out setup will allow you to use the surface water from the stream or pond to drive the ram that pumps the springwater to the home. The double acting ram is a device that I still marvel at to this day.

My Rife Ram has been running faithfully for over seventeen years and when I take a walk in the woods I tend to gravitate over to it to make sure all is well. The hydraulic ram pump is my favorite "old-school" solution for pumping water in a sustainable low cost way. Here is an example of how a ram system is laid out. Water is collected and directed to a ram via a drive pipe. The ram then lifts the water to an elevated cistern for storage. The system runs 24/7.

RIFE RIVER PUMP

River Pump

When it comes to streams that do not have enough fall to run a ram, then a river pump can be used. The river pump is a self-supporting system for pumping water. It is completely mechanical and operates without electricity or fuel. The power to drive is provided by flowing water. There is only one moving part, the swivel coupling, and it is water lubricated. All parts are noncorrosive and designed to withstand a high degree of stress. There is virtually no maintenance. Water pumped by the Rife River Pump can be used for household needs, irrigation, ponds, and gardening. It is especially useful in aerating stock tanks and fish tanks since it pumps half water and half air.

The river pump will pump all year through flash floods and frost. In areas with severe winters and danger of damage from floating ice floes, the river pump must be removed from operation during the cold months.

Windpump

Of course we cannot forget the windmill pump or the windpump. In the late 1880s and early 1900s, windmills were scattered all over the American landscape. They were indispensable to the settlers who were forced to move farther west to the sun-parched remote plains, after all the more desirable spots near rivers and streams had been taken. In the Great Plains and the vast territory known as the Great American Desert, water was more precious than gold. About one million windmills are pumping water

WINDMILL PUMP
(THOMAS CONLON,
IRON MAN
WINDMILL CO.
LTD.)

in the world today. The most common application is to install a windmill directly over a drilled or dug well. Pumping water from an aboveground source is also an easy task for a windmill. If you need to pump water on your property and the site has access to reliable winds, a water-pumping windmill may be a good option.

Bailer Bucket

As you can see water delivery requires some planning. If there is a power outage, it will not be long before any stored water is depleted. We encourage you to start with simple solutions for acquiring water and I will leave you with one of the simplest, a bailer bucket. It is the old-fashioned technique

where you use a rope and bucket that will fit into your well and you simply lower it to gather the water. Like most preparations you will need to test whether or not this will work on your water source. Many wells, especially in the Southeast, are top-discharge plumbing and access to the water requires that you remove the existing well pump.

PURIFICATION

It is of utmost importance to control the quality of your own water sources. Dehydration ensues rapidly when potable water is unavailable. If contaminated surface water is consumed, symptoms of dysentery can start within hours, which is debilitating at best, and lethal at worst. We recommend having at least three methods of treatment to make water potable.

Water Treatment Options

- Chemical
- Filtration

HOW TO DISINFECT WATER USING HIGH-TEST CALCIUM HYPOCHLORITE

1. Add and dissolve one teaspoonful of high-test granular calcium hypochlorite for each two gallons of water or for every 5 milliliters per 7.5 liters of water. *Do not drink this mixture.* The mixture will make a stock chlorine solution of approximately 500 milligrams per liter.

2. Store out of direct sunlight in a sealed container. The solution should be discarded after fourteen days.

3. To disinfect the water add the chlorine solutions in the ratio of 1 part chlorine solution to each 100 parts of water to be treated. This is approximately 1 pint of chlorine solution to every 12.5 gallons of water or .5 liter of solution to each 50 liters of water to be disinfected.

4. Shake or stir and then let the mixture rest for at least one hour before drinking. If the temperature is above 60 degrees Fahrenheit, wait a little while longer.

5. A slight chlorine odor will be present. To remove the smell, aerate the disinfected water by pouring it back and forth between clean containers.

- Reverse osmosis

- UV

- Heating

- SODIS

- Distillation

Chemical Treatment

Nearly all first world residents are familiar with the chlorine taste in water from municipal sources. Municipal sources typically use 72 percent calcium hypochlorite. This can be purchased in the form of pool shock.

When it comes to using chlorine bleach like Clorox to treat water, make sure it is unscented and not the "splashless" type. Use no more than twelve drops per gallon for untreated water. Let it sit thirty to forty-five minutes. Bleach loses its strength over time at roughly a rate of 50 percent per year. Granulated pool shock can be stored for years in a dry, cool place. Make sure you keep it away from metal as it is caustic.

Iodine tablets are a convenient way to treat water. These premeasured dissolvable tabs are intended for short-term or limited-emergency use only. Each tablet contains tetraglycine hydroperiodide (TGHP), which liberates titratable iodine when released into water. Tetraglycine hydroperiodide has great shelf life.

Filtration

Filtration is a method for removing bacteria, cysts, and viruses from the water supply. For the most part, the main concern with water sources is bacterial, but as water supplies become more contaminated, virus removal becomes important. Ceramic filters are popular for removing bacteria and cysts. The ceramic material is manufactured to a 0.1 to 0.2 micron pore size. The smallest bacteria are 0.2 micron in diameter. These filters are available in all sizes from portable straws up to whole-house systems. There are do-it-yourself bucket kits as well as stainless steel gravity-fed countertop units. All filters have a capacity limit, so plan accordingly. There are also membrane filters that can filter millions of gallons and can be back-flushed, such as Sawyer products. The newest development is in nanotechnology filters, where the pore size is at 0.01 micron. The smallest virus that causes human disease is the polio virus at 0.025 micron. I recommend the Sawyer system because it is inexpensive, produces more water than any other filter out there, and the product is made in America. However, with this system you need to add a bucket, and a hole must be drilled to accept the filter connections. The Berkey is also a quality made system; it looks nice and functions well with fewer added components and less work.

Filtration is the easiest, fastest method to produce potable water. I

**SAWYER MINI WATER
FILTRATION SYSTEM**

**BERKEY COUNTERTOP
WATER FILTER**

recommend having a personal filter in the car or bug-out bag for each member of the family, plus a gravity filter in a centralized location in your retreat.

Reverse Osmosis

Reverse Osmosis requires considerable energy and for that reason is not something I routinely recommend. I would consider it if I lived near the ocean, as it and distillation are the only ways to get salt out of salt water to make it potable.

Ultraviolet

Ultraviolet light treats water differently than the above methods. These UV rays alter the DNA of bacteria, cysts, and viruses thus rendering them sterile. They pass harmlessly through the GI tract, unable to infect the consumer. SteriPENs are an outstanding example of portable water treatment. These pens can purify sixteen ounces of water (cold or warm) in less than a minute and can be used up to eight thousand times.

SODIS

SODIS is a more passive purification method currently used in third world countries. It relies on exposure to ultraviolet rays over time to kill bacteria. Water-filled clear plastic bottles are often used with this method. The sealed plastic containers are placed in sunlight for about six hours.

Heating

A tried-and-true method of water treatment is boiling. Boiling is a safe method to treat water. Bring the water to a roiling boil for one minute, keeping in mind some water will evaporate. Let cool before drinking. One caveat: This method consumes a lot of energy. Boiled water tastes flat, so put oxygen back into it by pouring between two clean containers. This will also improve the taste of stored water. A safer way to ensure pasteurization takes place is to use a WAPI (Water Pasteurization Indicator). WAPIs are small plastic tubes with industrial grade wax inside of them that melts when water is heated to 150 °F for more than fifteen seconds.

| Use clean PET bottles | Fill bottles with water, and close the cap | Expose bottles to direct sunlight for at least 6 hours (or for two days under very cloudy conditions) | Store water in the SODIS bottles | Drink SODIS water directly from the bottles, or from clean cups |

SODIS PURIFICATION PROCESS

The SPADE (Solar PAsteurization DEtector) invented by Hydromissions International is a tough, shock-resistant, reusable capsule and wing nut. Wax melts at 160 °F with a flow at 165 °F. Note: This is a temperature (not biological) indicator only, and is *not* the same as SODIS (UV).

Distillation

Distillation is a process where water is converted to steam and captured by a series of tubes. Distillation not only kills most microbes, but it removes them as well as heavy metals, salts, and other chemicals from the water. It is time-consuming with a small yield for the amount of energy required. In most disasters access to energy is limited.

Conclusion

In summary, a lack of clean water will drive you out of your shelter quickly. You must have control over your potable water source. This is why it is imperative that you store water. Having a water plan in place should be the top priority in any type of disaster preparedness. Continually work on ways to resupply water to your location and have redundant methods for treating water.

FOOD

Store What You Eat—
Eat What You Store

Eighty percent of the people in the world have no food safety net.
When disaster strikes—the economy gets blown, people lose a job,
floods, war, conflict, bad governance, all of those things—
there is nothing to fall back on.

—Josette Sheeran, former Executive Director of the UN World Food Programme

After water, food is the next most important resource for any prepper. Without an adequate food supply you will not be able to stay in your location for very long, placing the survival of both yourself and your loved ones in jeopardy. Most folks have just a few days' worth of food in their homes.

Practical Preppers Recommends a Threefold Approach to Your Food Plan:

- Storage
- Resupply
- Preservation

FOOD STORAGE

Food storage is priority one when it comes to a disaster plan. Many people underestimate its importance, believing they will be able to purchase what they need just before an event occurs. Or they believe that all services will be restored within a day or two, so why bother. Others say they will just grow what they will need or because they have guns and ammo they will just hunt for food. Growing food is time-intensive, requires ongoing physical labor, and, since crop cultivation is seasonal, requires many variables working together. Hunting is another valuable food-storage option. During typical circumstances, there is a multitude of readily available ammunition available in America. But, as the ammo shortage of early 2013 taught us, a single high-profile tragedy such as the Sandy Hook shooting or talk of gun-control legislation can quickly result in bare store shelves and steep price increases. The decimation of the animal population is another situational scenario that also must be considered when relying primarily on hunting to put food on the table. I believe that many folks realize grocery stores can be stripped clean quickly, but at the same time too many take for granted that services will be restored quickly. When there is word of the slightest chance of snowstorms or hurricanes, milk and bread are among the first items to disappear from supermarket shelves. I live in a rural county in the Southeastern United States and only 1 percent of the food needed for the population is grown in our county. In the United States, food is mainly supplied by the trucking industry. This industry can easily come to a screeching halt if a variety of man-made or natural disasters occur. Many retailers such as Walmart and Amazon are piloting programs that deliver "fresh" food right to your door. That is an amazing convenience, but it could lull millions of families into yet another layer of dependence. Imagine all your groceries ordered on your phone and delivered next day and placed in your refrigerator and freezer. A glitch on the power grid will bring this fragile supply chain to its knees. Realistically, just one of these possible scenarios clearly illustrates why food storage is nonnegotiable.

Entire books are dedicated to food-storage lists, but the general rule is to buy and store the kinds of foods that your family likes to eat. I would also add that leaning toward foods that are easy to prepare will be beneficial in a crisis situation. Don't forget the manual can openers! The question of how long a person can live without food is a complicated one. The easy answer, and the one most cited in a quick web search, is thirty to forty days. However, this quick answer does not address activity level, stress level, and amount of extra weight when that last bite was taken. In disaster preparedness, nutrition and calories are very important as activity and stress levels are extremely high. Also, how well an individual can survive the initial event is often dependent on the individual's fitness level. When I look at a client's overall food storage, I look for three tiers of nutritional preparedness:

- Short term (for initial shock phase)
- Long term (for return to rule of law, but before trade and shipping commence)
- Vitamin and oil storage (for nutritional boost)

Short-Term Food Storage

The shortest of course is what is in the refrigerator. These perishables only have a few days at most before becoming unfit and dangerous to eat, and should be considered first. A freezer without power will also be useless within five to seven days, unless you have planned ahead and have a separate circuit on generator or solar power. Vacuum sealed and canned food will last several months so that can be mixed in with other long-term foods. MREs (Meals Ready to Eat) are a great choice to store for short-term use. They can be kept at various temperatures, although a stable temperature will yield the most nutritional product in the long term. Most food studies show storing such items between 60 to 70 degrees Fahrenheit is the ideal range. It is always preferable to store what you like to eat. Choose items with a long shelf life so the food can be rotated from storage to the kitchen cabinet before the expiration date and provide a balanced diet.

Short-Term Food-Storage List

- Canned or dehydrated vegetables
- Canned or dehydrated meat, fish, and poultry
- Canned or dehydrated fruit
- Vitamin supplements
- Canned or dehydrated dairy products such as eggs and milk
- Comfort foods to serve as morale boosters
- MREs

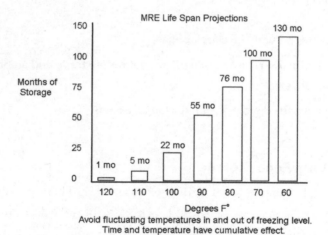

MRE Life Span Projections

Avoid fluctuating temperatures in and out of freezing level.
Time and temperature have cumulative effect.

MRE LIFESPAN

MREs Were Originally Developed for the Armed Services. Currently, an MRE consists of:

- ENTRÉE—the main course, such as spaghetti or beef stew
- SIDE DISH—rice, corn, fruit, or mashed potatoes, etc.
- CRACKERS OR BREAD

CASE OF MRES

- **SPREAD**—peanut butter, jelly, or cheese spread

- **DESSERT**—cookies or pound cakes

- **CANDY**—M&Ms, Skittles, or Tootsie Rolls

- **BEVERAGES**—Gatorade-like mixes, cocoa, dairy shakes, coffee, tea

- **HOT SAUCE OR SEASONING**—in some MREs

- **FLAMELESS RATION HEATER**—to heat the entrée

- **ACCESSORIES**—spoon, matches, creamer, sugar, salt, chewing gum, toilet paper, etc.

Each MRE provides an average of 1,250 calories (13 percent protein, 36 percent fat, and 51 percent carbohydrates) and one-third of the military Recommended Dietary Allowance (RDA) of vitamins and minerals. A full day's worth of meals would consist of three MREs.

MREs also, since they are completely self-contained, can be given as charity to neighbors. They taste best when heated as directed. It is also important to store some type of laxative with them. MREs contain almost no fiber and this is done on purpose, as elimination can occur spontaneously in some individuals during high stress. Notice the energy level: 3,750 calories on average for a day's worth of meals. These meals were developed and studied for use in highly active, fit, stressed individuals. I usually advise storing seven days' worth (twenty-one meals) of meals per person to be stored as the minimum number of MREs to keep on hand.

Long-Term Food Storage

Freeze-dried and dehydrated foods are excellent choices for long-term storage. They require only dry, cool conditions and will last for fifteen years or more. There are many companies in the United States that supply these foods in #10 cans and pouches. Pouches are great for portability, but being soft-sided they can be punctured. The #10 cans are larger but store neatly in boxes and can be stacked. DIYers can also acquire food-grade buckets and use either Mylar bags or gamma lids (lids with airtight seal) and oxygen absorbers and prepare beans, grains, livestock food, or other foods themselves. Many companies, like Mountain House, offer prepared meals as well as individual foods in prepackaged containers. The prepared meals (most similar to camping meals—just add hot water) are higher in price but in return offer convenience and speed. Do take the time to read the labels from a calorie standpoint as it is difficult to store enough calories for active, stressed people in only three meals. If the size of the meal is only 500 calories, you will need to store other foods, like freeze-dried fruit, for snacks. I usually recommend twenty-one days' worth (sixty-three meals, plus snacks) per person to be stored as a minimum number of prepared freeze-dried/dehydrated meals. The logic behind this is that

---

WHAT IS A #10 CAN?

When referring to a #10 can, think of a metal can of coffee that you might see at your local grocery stores. Or, if you ever worked in the food industry, you might have had the opportunity to see a #10 can in the back room. The term *#10* does not reference that the contents will weigh 10 pounds; the #10 denotes the ability to hold an equivalent amount of 109.43 ounces. One gallon is 128 ounces.

the catastrophe, now in its second week, has started to gain some order. Any individuals still at the scene are prepared and are able to heat water.

Storing individual foods such as beans and grain for long-term use requires extra considerations. Dry beans are nearly impossible to eat without cooking. Attempting to consume beans raw can cause harm to the digestive tract. I find most people who are storing massive amounts of beans have not taken into consideration the massive amount of fuel needed to cook them for the necessary eight to twelve hours. Similarly, whole grain such as wheat berries must be run through a grain mill to be turned into flour to be used for bread. Manual hand mills should be considered as most disasters have power disruptions so no electricity other than what the individual can make should be counted on. It is also impor-tant to remember that freeze-dried foods should be reconstituted with water prior to consuming. Eating dried foods without proper water intake will cause water to be pulled from the bloodstream if there is insufficient water in the intestines to rehydrate the food. In the worst of scenarios, intestinal obstruction can occur from the partially rehydrated food.

The last component of long-term storage is the freeze-dried individ-ual foods. This is for when some normalcy has been restored but there are still shortages of trucked supplies (food, medicine, clothes). This is where more involved recipes and actual cooking can start to take place. These foods can be put together to look like a familiar American plate—a meat plus two or three sides. A word of warning: Many "one year supply for one person" offers are calorically restricted, usually 2,000 calories per day or less. In addition, they often contain large amounts of staples, primarily sugar and flour. These offers are calculated solely on calories: A #10 can of sugar contains 12,000 calories—and absolutely no nutrition. Also, the fruit drink most often offered is flavored sugar, perhaps with some vitamin C. The "meat" offered in these is scanty—usually flavored textured vegetable protein (TVP) is substituted for actual beef or chicken. If you have never tried TVP, be warned that it can be difficult to digest. Many people feel gaseous and bloated after eating it. I encourage folks to buy a few cans or pouches and try the products before investing in a larger supply. Also, for this stage, it is worth the trouble to make a seven-day menu that rotates and purchase the individual components needed to prepare the meals.

Meal Options Commonly Sold by Long-Term Food-Storage Suppliers

- Breakfast meals that contain bacon, eggs, pancake mix, and oatmeal

- Meat-based dishes such as lasagna, beef stroganoff, and chili

- Soup meals that often include beef stew, chicken noodle soup, and potato cheddar soup

- Snack packets that could contain tropical fruit medley and almond coconut granola

- Pasta dishes and casserole meals that often include chicken or vegetarian options

- Milk and whey milk sold by the case

- Bread, muffin, and biscuit mix packets or buckets

- Buckets of flour and sugar

- Juice and flavored milk mixes

Vitamin and Nutrient Recommendations

Vitamin A	5000 IU
Vitamin B1	1.5 mg
Vitamin B2	1.7 mg
Vitamin B3	20 mg NE1
Vitamin B6	2 mg
Vitamin B12	6 mcg
Vitamin C	60 mg
Vitamin D	400 IU
Vitamin E	30 IU
Vitamin K	80 mcg
Biotin	300 mcg
Calcium	1000 mg
Copper	2 mg
Folic Acid	400 mcg
Iodine	150 mcg
Iron	18 mg
Magnesium	400 mg
Manganese	2 mg
Pantothenic Acid	10 mg
Phosphorus	1000 mg
Zinc	15 mg

VITAMIN AND NUTRIENT RECOMMENDATIONS

Vitamins and Oils

These are overlooked but vital additions to food storage. Vitamin deficiencies can occur within just a few weeks. Scurvy, the lack of vitamin C, is a serious deficiency characterized by poor appetite, exhaustion, ulcerated gums, and loss of teeth. Because humans cannot synthesize vitamin C, we normally get it as an additive in our regular foods and from fresh foods. Any average multivitamin contains enough vitamin C to prevent scurvy. Most B vitamins are also in fresh food, as well as vitamin A in green leafy vegetables. Essential fatty acids (EFAs) are also vital and deficiency in them becomes obvious within three to four weeks. Examples of these are EPA, ALA, and DHA, which are types of omega-3 fatty acids. These fats are required for biological processes and are not just fuel. Symptoms of deficiency include fatigue, poor memory, dry skin, and heart problems. Sources of EFAs are whole grains, fresh fruits/vegetables, fish, and olive oil. Canned sardines, salmon, and tuna, and olive oil should also be considered as long-term food-storage staples. Refer to the USDA chart of recommended daily amounts of vitamins and nutrients to determine the supply needed for use by your family. The chart will be highly useful when choosing the types of foods to place in both your long- and short-term storage supply.

Vitamin and Oil Storage List

- Multivitamins
- EFAs (supplements such as fish oil capsules, olive oil, canned sardines, salmon, tuna)

Comfort Foods

This category of foods addresses the psychological component of facing a disaster. In high-stress situations, many people resort to high-sugar treats to cope with the situation. Also, children who are used to highly processed meals from fast-food restaurants will be overwhelmed when plain oatmeal is what is on the menu. I once had a client who had a nice solution to address this issue for her grandchildren. She purchased sugary breakfast cereals and placed them in her quart canning jars. She also had a manual brake bleeder with a psi gauge and FoodSaver vacuum sealing accessory. She placed a rubber lid on each jar and the jar sealer over it, and then attached the hose end of the brake bleeder to the top of the jar sealer and manually pumped the air out of the jar. The psi gauge rose accordingly, and she stopped when the gauge read 10 psi. This also has worked well at our house for dry cookies (store-bought) and crackers. We have found the food still is crispy at one year. Of course, the brake bleeder must be dedicated to this (brake fluid should not be near food), and certainly the entire FoodSaver vacuum sealing system could be used to do this. The important takeaway in this is a dry-pack method for foods with high sugar content and low moisture. This technique should not be used to replace

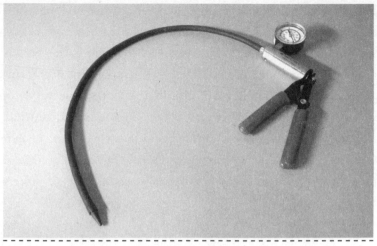

BRAKE BLEEDER

wet pack canning, i.e., jams and pickles. The jars are already made to be used over and over, and extra lids take very little room and last for years in storage.

Many women ask my wife how to store chocolate for long periods of time. We have found the cocoa butter separates and forms a white dusty coating on the outside of the bars when we have tried to store them, even at 70 degrees Fahrenheit. The favorite at our house is Nutella, a chocolate hazelnut spread. It generally has a manufacturer's expiration date of eighteen months and can be used like peanut butter. It does have tree nuts in it, so a word of caution to those with allergies. We have also dry-packed (#10 can) plain M&Ms. We opened them at eighteen months (no oxygen absorber was used) and they were in very good condition. The candy shell seems to prohibit melting and the white coating from forming.

Palate Fatigue

Many are unfamiliar with this term or concept. *Palate fatigue* refers to a situation in which the same food is offered repeatedly to an individual. This issue arises when the individual develops revulsion to the food, preferring not to eat. This can occur in the military; early statistics on MREs indicated 40 percent of the meal was not ingested—this is no longer the case due to increased variety. It is one of the primary reasons why variety is so important, especially to children. Also, if all that you have stored is rice and beans, it will become more difficult to consume each day. Eating the same food day in and day out will not only potentially decrease morale but will also not allow the body to obtain all the proper nutrients. A well-balanced diet becomes even more important when increased energy is needed to accomplish the enhanced physical labor you will be doing during either a short- or long-term disaster. Foods high in protein are strongly recommended.

FOOD RESUPPLY

Most of us currently use a market as our resupply plan for our food and hygiene products. But what if the stores were closed? Or empty? A well-thought-out resupply plan can bring peace-filled self-reliance. Stored food

WINTER GARDENING

can get you through tough times but if at all possible, begin to develop your food resupply plan. It will take a lot of time and hard work but the payback is great when you can complement stored food with fresh milk, eggs, fish, salads, and bread.

Orchard

Even on a small piece of property, fruit and nut trees and bushes can flourish. The standard size tree, growing forty feet or more, is easily replaced by a semidwarf or dwarf tree. There are even grafted trees that have two or three branches with different fruit on each. When selecting a species of tree or bush to plant, the growing zone must be considered. Oranges do not grow in cold climates. A tree's root system will extend at least to where the leaf canopy stops, so consider underground pipes or leech fields for septic tanks when placing the plant. A southern exposure will give the tree maximal light. Check out one of the many books dedicated to fruiting perennial plantings, or consult with a local agricultural extension or gardener as to particulars of your growing region.

Garden

Gardening usually refers to growing annual plants that bear a crop, such as tomatoes, green beans, squash, peppers, and others that may be common to your growing region. Gardening fosters self-reliance and is a relatively cheap way to produce food. There are, again, many books and individuals dedicated to this subject. One of the first resources to consult is the hardiness map for the country and many maps are available by county or province. The growing zone map is the standard by which gardeners and growers can determine which plants are most likely to thrive at a location.

There are many styles of gardening. Some standard examples include traditional single rows, wide rows, intensive planting in blocks, raised beds, level beds . . . the list goes on. You may want to incorporate paths in the garden, especially if it's large, and tillers, cultivators, and wheelbarrows are needed. You may want to use mulch so you can do less weeding and watering. Garden plans are definitely not "one size fits all." Some plants

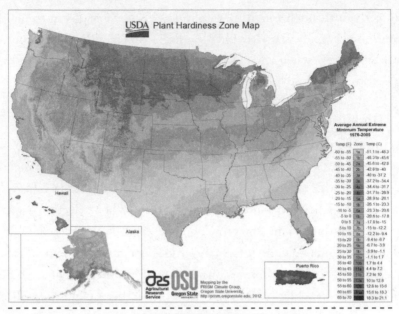

GARDEN GROWING ZONES
(AGRICULTURAL RESEARCH SERVICE, U.S. DEPARTMENT OF AGRICULTURE)

thrive when they are planted close together, and some plants like tomatoes need their space. What will work for you will greatly depend upon the space you have to work with and its exposure to sunlight. Start small so that you don't become overwhelmed by the sheer amount of weeding and cultivation required. I grew up working on a dairy farm that also had about twenty acres of row crop vegetables. I looked down those endless rows and with my hoe in hand hardly got to the end of one after a day of proper cultivation and weeding. I am glad I was exposed to the old-school methods that required simple tools and perseverance so that I know what it is like to cultivate without modern (grid-dependent) appliances. Experiment with different garden styles now and find out what works for you.

I offer my clients gardening recommendations based upon past successes and failures. If you have the room, fence in as large an area as possible for growing food. This will give you room to turn a tractor and to store compost piles, garden sheds, stakes, watering equipment, and other garden accessories. Think big but start small! Good crop production is

POTATOES
(MCKAY SAVAGE)

based on good soils. If you are a gardener you are first a soil maker. Composting and access to natural fertilizer is a plus. Utilizing "high gardening soil amendments" like Biochar will greatly improve soil quality and its yield. I have met and talked to a lot of folks who have seed supplies but their soil has never been touched, turned, or worked. These individuals are in for a rude awakening that first year of planting. Getting rid of the established grasses and weeds alone will be hard work. I always try to make it a priority to add a little bit of cultivated land each year on my property. By using this process, if I am ever forced to work it by hand, I am ahead of the curve. Having a large pile of decomposing biomass is so helpful in amending the garden. A rich soil full of the right mixture of soil, organic matter, Biochar, and worms is very rewarding. But remember, not every veggie is going to like the same mixture so do your homework and practice.

Grains

When it comes to producing grains, like barley, wheat, and oats, many of the same rules as gardening apply. Know what will thrive in your area before purchasing seeds or plants. Some experimentation might be in order. I wanted to plant hard red spring wheat on my property, but not owning a combine, a sickle bar, or a thresher, I set out to do everything by hand on a 1.5-acre wheat plot. Why? I wanted to experience growing my own wheat, harvesting it, storing it, and having enough to do it all over again the following year.

My Experience with Growing, Harvesting, and Storing Wheat

I told some friends and family members what I was doing and a few said they wanted to help as they were curious. I tilled the ground and broadcast the certified organic wheat berries that I purchased at a rate of 120 pounds per acre. I planted it about two weeks prior to when corn is planted in my area. The germination rate was fantastic and the entire plot came to life in about two weeks. I was very happy with how the wheat was looking

BROADCASTER

HEADS OF WHEAT

but I was also wondering how in the world I was going to turn this field into bread and save enough back for the following year. This same thought process needs to be played out when it comes to corn, barley, and oats. I figured that if I could grow forty bushels per acre I would have at least a ton of wheat berries after all the waste and mistakes in getting it to its final storage space.

Once the wheat was mature and ready for harvest, I did borrow a sickle bar mower from a friend but we could have used the traditional farm scythe. Since that time I have added a couple of scythes to the tool inventory. The sickle bar worked great. The day I decided to cut, I enlisted a bunch of helpers to gather and bundle the wheat into sheaths and stack them in the field in the sun to finish drying. Once that was complete, I could tell I was losing my helpers as it was hard work. I loaded all the wheat on a trailer and brought it to the barn, but I wasn't sure how I was going to thresh it. Threshing is the process of removing the wheat berries from the hull and rest of the plant. I tried a wood chipper and thought I had something but it wasn't the best. I tried laying the wheat on the ground and beating it with a short piece of water hose—that labor-intensive task was going nowhere. I finally tried driving on it with my tractor and that worked great. I threshed all the wheat this way.

I also used an industrial fan to winnow the wheat, separating it from the chaff. I threw the wheat in the air and the chaff, being lighter, blew away. I ended up with a lot of wheat and little help. I was the only one still excited that I was able to make bread from my own property. It took hours to clean the wheat and even my finished product had stems and chaff in it. I began to dream about owning a combine. When it came to storage, my wife had picked up a lot of frosting buckets from a local grocery store, so we put the wheat in them and then in our basement. We also took some wheat and put it in our freezer for three days to kill the wheat weevils and then stored that in the same gasketed frosting buckets. Both stored extremely well and we still have some high quality wheat after five years of storage. I still had about four bushels left over that I wanted to set aside for chicken feed, and that is when I found out a better way to produce

AFTER THE THRESHING

chicken food. I had put the wheat in a 55-gallon drum and stored it in my barn. I thought I would get really clever by sealing the drum and adding a vacuum fitting, but never got around to that. One day, after a few months of storage, I noticed a noise coming from the barrel so I of course decided to open it. It was alive! It was crawling with wheat weevils and the eggs they laid in the wheat had turned to larvae. The larvae were about one-inch in length and there was a ton of them. This incredibly disgusting vat of weevils and worms fed my chickens through the winter. The egg production was amazing since their new wiggly feed was solid protein. I had found a solution to keeping my chickens fed during times when they could not get enough food by free ranging or from our food scraps. The chickens loved their new diet and looked forward to feeding time. Once the life cycle process of the wheat weevil was in full swing I added other sources of food for them to process. This included some more wheat, vegetable scraps from the garden, and even carcasses of rodents that I trapped. Everything was turned into worms for the chickens.

Back to Bread

It is very rewarding to be able to take your own grain and process it into enjoyable food for the family. This is my wife's area of expertise. One major step of course is in grinding the wheat berries into flour. Since we had so much wheat to grind, I was not going to settle on a poorly made wheat grinder so I purchased a Country Living Grain Mill and have gotten great service from it. The design of this mill utilizes an exercise bike and that is how we grind our wheat today. I have a video of this on our Engineer 775 Practical Preppers YouTube channel.

Tools for the Garden

There are many amazing power tools for the garden. For large gardens it is hard to beat a compact or subcompact tractor. Tractors with loaders and their plethora of possible attachments will spoil you in a hurry but make quick work out of soil preparation. I have been keeping track of diesel fuel consumption for early spring garden plot preparation and I can prep one acre of soil with about one gallon of diesel fuel. The best combination I have found to prepare a food plot is to use a set of scarifiers that penetrate deep in to the ground, loosening that soil. I then put on the rototiller and finish off the plot. The result is a beautifully prepared garden plot that you hate to actually even walk in. However, I recommend you obtain as many different hand tools as you can find for the variety of gardening tasks.

Vegetable Garden Tool List

- **DIGGING FORK**—Some would call this tool a gardener's favorite tool, but it is really your soil's best friend. Great for turning the soil, aeration, and mixing nutrients into the soil.

- **DIGGING SPADE**—Great for digging, turning the soil, soil aeration, and its straight blade also makes it a good edging tool.

- **HOES**—The never-ending battle with weeds is best tackled with a hoe or cultivator. There are many, many head shapes available and most gardeners have a favorite.

- **RAKE**—If you're making a new garden or adding on to an existing plot, the garden rake is great for leveling and clearing debris from your soil.

- **HAND TOOLS**—Now that you have the workhorse tools, you may find any number of smaller tools handy when you're out in the garden. These tools will probably be specific to your type of gardening.

- **PRUNERS**—Every gardener's go-to pruning tool—buy a good pair and you'll have a lifetime garden tool.

- **CULTIVATORS**—A cultivator will help you aerate soil and kill weeds. There are several different types of manual-wheeled cultivators. Many of them have a variety of attachments and are a must-have as an alternative to the gas-powered devices.

Saving Seeds

Growing crops that will yield in the soil type and temperature zone where you dwell is an integral part of sustainable gardening. Many people preparing for disruptions in food supply are adamant on storing heirloom seeds. It is important for the newcomer to know there is a difference between hybrid and nonhybrid seed.

Hybrid seed is seed that is made by crossing two different plants within the same species that typically have a greater crop yield than either plant separately. This is a good thing, but only for the first year. Should the seed from that hybrid plant be saved, it is not genetically "true." In other words, when that saved seed is planted the following year, the crop yield will not be the same as the year before. The yield is greatly reduced, or

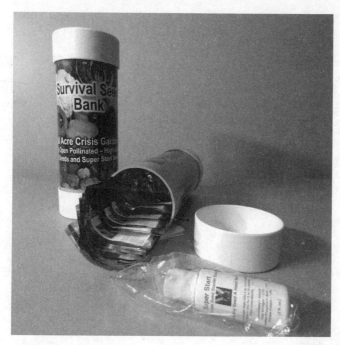

worse, nonexistent. This keeps the patent safe for the companies who produce the hybrid seed. The consumer must purchase the seed every year to get the high yield expected. Heirloom, or nonhybrid, seed breeds "true" each year, as long as the genetic line is not contaminated by another local crop. Heirlooms in general do not have quite as high a yield as a hybrid; however, the seed can be saved each year. Again, there are books dedicated to the process of saving seed. Seeds must come from a fully mature fruit. Also, contamination can occur when wind or bees, depending on how the crop is pollinated, carry pollen from a nearby garden with a different strain of crop. I have saved heirloom seeds with varying degrees of success. I do encourage folks who have a garden resupply plan to store both types. Hybrids bear heavily and are frequently bred to resist plant infections common in the type of plant they are. Heirlooms are more susceptible to infection. Hybrid seed lasts two to five years, with percent

SMALL GREENHOUSE

germination dropping with each successive year. Heirloom seeds have reportedly been stored for many years.

Greenhouses

These buildings can extend the growing season substantially. They also require some power to run large fans that circulate the air. Also consider that approximately 85 percent of food grown requires bees to pollinate, so you will either want to hand pollinate or make adjustments to allow bees access to the greenhouse.

CATTLE

Livestock

Poultry, rabbits, goats, and cows all require a bit more room and some tolerant neighbors. Check first with your local ordinances, as many subdivisions have rules about what constitutes a pet. Another consideration in disaster planning is how you will care for your animals in a catastrophic situation. What if they get loose? Do you have enough food and water stored for them? What can you do if their shelter is destroyed? In rural living, these answers may be simple. In suburban areas, however, a loose, frightened animal will most likely be viewed as a danger or a meal (for someone else). Certainly storing extra fencing, post, and wire can be a solution. Taking on the responsibility of livestock usually means evacuation is not the preferred decision in the face of disaster. Remember to check with your insurance carrier about adding new coverage to include damage caused by livestock should they become loose. I once had a young heifer break through my fencing along the road and she was hit by a car.

CHICKENS

If I hadn't had coverage it would have been a very costly expense. I was fortunate that the driver wasn't hurt, all damages were covered, and I was even paid for the cow that died. We were able to save the meat as well.

Livestock are a critical part of a resupply plan and essential if your goal is some level of self-sufficiency. In order to reach this goal, some variant of what was called *high farming* in Europe has to be implemented. This is a balance between animals and plants, so that each feeds the other. The plants are used to feed the animals directly and the animals are used to feed the soil with their manure. We are seeing this concept catching on in the area of aquaponics as well. When clients are working through the livestock-purchasing decision-making process, I tell folks to start small, both in number and type. I am a big fan of dual-purpose animals. Animals such as chickens that can provide both eggs and meat are a great place to begin. Larger animals such as Jersey dairy cows bred to beef bulls can provide both meat and dairy products. Just as when determining what seeds to plant in your garden, make sure you raise livestock that will thrive in your area. I have found that cows that have low birth weights, are disease resistant, and can actually put on weight in the hot summers are what's best for me, as opposed to a purebred line that produces a large beautiful animal, but the vet bills and loss rate at birth are way too high. Some folks like rabbits because they are silent, prolific, and require little space to raise. They also have the highest feed-to-protein conversion of any livestock you can raise.

Rotating Livestock

Just as you rotate your gardens to alleviate soil depletion you want to rotate your livestock often. This requires planning in regard to your fencing and water distribution. There are some amazing advances in intensive grazing that actually use the animal to make better soil. Some call this *trampling* or *mob grazing*. How it works: You take your herd and confine them to small paddocks long enough for the grass to be completely flattened; then you move them to the next one. This causes the grass to compost and the soil thrives. By the time the cows come around to that section again, it is reseeded and grown up to where they do it all over again. The benefits are amazing in terms of a smaller space requirement and then, in some regions, there is no need for tractors to process hay. Year-round rotational grazing just makes sense.

Different Breeds for Different Forages

When it comes to livestock, most breeds eat specific forages and sometimes it is nice to have a couple of types of animals that complement each other through their diet. For example, grazing goats and cattle cohabitate together well and will produce more meat per acre than grazing either species alone. Cattle and goats prefer different species of forages. Goats will eat many species of plants that cattle will not eat such as sprouts, greenbrier, hackberry, black berry, ragweed, golden rod, kudzu, and lespedeza. In pastures stocked only with cattle these plants become "weeds" robbing the cattle forages of moisture and nutrients. Because they are not grazed, they flourish and take over the pasture. Unless these weeds are controlled the land becomes less productive each year. They can be controlled with chemical herbicides but the herbicides are expensive. They also require expensive labor and fuel to apply. The herbicides can be harmful to the environment and might even be harmful to the livestock and to those consuming the meat. On the other hand, when goats are placed on these pastures the weeds become forages for goats, and they no longer flourish out of control.

Internal parasites (stomach worms) are a major problem with goats. While cattle are more resistant to internal parasites than goats, parasites do lower gains in cattle. The parasites that infect cattle do not infect goats and those that infect goats do not infect cattle. Thus grazing both cattle and goats on the same land not only reduces the grazing pressure on the favorite forages for each species, but also reduces parasite contamination

ESTABLISHED WATER SOURCE

from each, making it easier to control parasites without worm medications. If worm medications are used too much, the parasites become resistant to them and the medications become less effective. Most worm medications also kill dung beetles, which clean up the droppings left by cattle and goats. Thus the medications have an adverse effect on the environment and might even have negative effects on the health of humans who eat the meat produced. The benefits from grazing both cattle and goats on the same pastures include more meat produced per acre, less money spent for weed and internal parasite control, less adverse effects of herbicides and worm medications on the environment, healthier livestock, and more nutritious meat produced.

Aquaponics

This specialized farming uses much less water than conventional gardening. It also requires some power for pumping water to keep it oxygenated, so I do encourage having a back-up method like a solar generator to run the pumps as required. It is a fine balance of fish, plants, worms, bacteria, and nitrogen. It is very rewarding to be able to create this balanced ecosystem that can produce all the vegetables and protein that you need. Production areas can range from patio size to large operations. There are many books dedicated to aquaponics.

An established pond on your property is a storehouse of food. From fish to turtles to frogs and edible plants a pond is a sustainable food resupplier. A pond can also provide a lot of recreation for the family. When constructing a pond, consider installing at least one line through the dam that can be used to supply the water and energy to run a ram pump. Make sure that the pond can be easily drained so that if you need to supplement your food stores with fresh food, you can drain the pond down, making it easier to net your fish. Even very small fish make for great fish patties once processed through a grinder.

A pond not only provides a lot of food but it is another way to store huge amounts of water that can be treated later. Make sure the species that you stock in your pond will flourish in your climate. Trying to raise trout in too warm a zone is a disaster and warm-weather fish will surely not make it above certain latitudes. Consult with your local farm extensions and fish hatcheries before beginning such a project. Occasionally feeding your established fish population with a floating fish food will give you an idea of how many fish are in your pond. It is not an exact science but helps determine when you might have to restock. Sometimes you have to deal with those competing "fisherman" such as turtles, cranes, herons, and neighborhood teenagers who find out that you have a really nice pond to "fish" in.

One of the best decisions I made on our property was installing a pond and I have plans for another. As I mentioned, the pond can generate enough energy to pump water to great heights using a ram pump, so I plan on using the first pond to fill an upper pond that is closer to the house where the fishing competition can be controlled. Research local codes and find a reputable pond builder who knows how to build a pond that will not leak, before beginning the construction process. Building a pond that will not leak can be a tricky thing to do in soils that are very porous. One old trick to seal your leaking pond is to unleash a herd of pigs into the pond—

they will work the soil and mud into the leaking crevices. Putting a liner in a pond is an outrageously expensive solution to a leaking pond. There are some nontoxic polymers on the market that have been used to seal leaking ponds with great success. Water$ave PL Plug is one of my favorite products to accomplish this task. By using the plug there is no need for expensive, heavy earth moving, pond drainage, or to begin a rebuilding project on an existing pond. The plug can also be applied either fully or partially on water-filled ponds and is environmentally friendly.

PRESERVATION

Now that we've established the sources of food, what can you do with the bounty? Preserve it! We live in a society dependent on big business to provide scrupulously clean preserved food. To preserve it ourselves, we must make safety the first priority. Also, using different methods will yield excellent products, depending on the food itself. Potatoes—are they better canned or from the root cellar? Meat—would you prefer soup or smoked ribs? Your goals can go beyond surviving; you can thrive in your self-reliant lifestyle if you plan properly.

Canning

Fresh food contains bacteria, molds, and yeast. Once it is placed in a vacuum, the environment is changed so that a potentially fatal level of bacteria anaerobes such as *Clostridium botulinum,* botulism, can grow. Always start with clean hands, food, and equipment. Using the correct canning process yields a sterile product and holds it in that state until you are ready to eat it. When looking at fruits and vegetables, the acidity of the food determines which process you use. Canning in a boiling water bath is appropriate for most fruits and pickled vegetables. You are able to can virtually any food item.

List of Foods to Can

- Meat, fish, and poultry
- Fruits
- Vegetables
- Milk
- Butter
- Dehydrated eggs

Water-Bath Canning

Boiling water-bath canning is a safe and economical method of preserving high acid foods. It has been used for decades especially by home gardeners and others interested in providing food storage for their families where quality control of the food is in one's own hands. Home food preservation also promotes a sense of personal satisfaction and accomplishment. The guesswork is taken out of providing a safe food supply that has been preserved at home when guidelines for operating a water-bath canner are followed exactly, scientifically tested/approved recipes are utilized (1988 or later), and good quality equipment, supplies, and produce are used.

What Foods Are Typically Processed Using a Boiling Water-Bath Method and Why?

High acid foods can be safely processed at temperatures reached in the boiling water-bath canner. To kill harmful molds, yeasts, and some bacteria, processing using the boiling water-bath method ensures the safety of the preserved produce. Foods such as fruits, pickles, sauerkraut, jams, jellies, marmalades, and fruit butters/spreads fit into the high acid group since they have an acidity, or pH level, of 4.6 or lower. Most tomatoes and tomato products also fit into this category provided current recommendations for acidification are followed.

Current recommendations for acidification of whole, crushed, or juiced tomatoes are to add 2 tablespoons of bottled lemon juice or $1/2$

teaspoon of citric acid per quart of tomatoes. For pints, use 1 tablespoon bottled lemon juice or ¹/₄ teaspoon citric acid. Four tablespoons of a 5 percent acidity vinegar per quart may be used instead of lemon juice or citric acid. However, vinegar may cause undesirable flavor changes. Add sugar (or salt) to offset acid taste, if desired. This does not affect the acidity of the tomatoes.

Become Familiar with the Parts of a Boiling Water-Bath Canner

The general method for water-bath canning is as follows:

1. Fill the canner halfway with water.

2. Preheat water to 140 °F for raw-packed foods and to 180 °F (simmering with steam) for hot-packed foods. Raw- or cold-packed foods are placed directly into hot jars and covered with hot syrup; hot-packed foods are partially cooked or heated through and placed hot into hot jars and covered with hot syrup. Use tested recipes with detailed instructions for various types of produce.

3. Load filled jars, fitted with lids, into the canner rack and use the handles to lower the rack into the water; or fill the canner, one jar at a time, with a jar lifter.

4. Add more boiling water, if needed, so the water level is at least one inch above jar tops.

5. Cover with the canner lid and turn heat to its highest position until water boils vigorously.

6. Set a timer for the number of minutes required for processing the food. (Check tested recipes for specific instructions for jams/ jellies and pickles.)

7. Lower the heat setting to maintain a gentle boil throughout the process schedule.

8. Add more boiling water, if needed, to keep the water level to above one inch of the jar lids.

9. When jars have been boiled for the recommended time, turn off the heat and remove the canner lid.

10. Using a jar lifter, remove the jars and place them on a protected surface, leaving at least one-inch spaces between the jars during cooling. Keep away from air drafts and let the jars cool at room temperature.

11. Label your filled jars, including the date processed, and store them (without the screw bands) in a cool, dark, dry place.

Pressure Canning

A pressure canner is required to kill the harmful bacteria in foods that lack acid such as vegetables and meat. The temperature of boiling water is 212 degrees Fahrenheit. The temperature in a pressure canner is 240 degrees Fahrenheit, at a minimum. Bacteria are destroyed in the temperature range of 165 to 240 degrees Fahrenheit. Since there is now so much good science in safe canning, buying a book with well-tested recipes means you don't reinvent the wheel. Food poisoning is a very real threat and a self-made catastrophe if cleanliness is ignored.

ALL AMERICAN
PRESSURE CANNER

CANNED FOOD SPOILAGE WARNING SIGNS

- MOLDY JAR—Perhaps the seal has broken, leading to leakage.

- DISCOLORED FOOD—The jar's contents are dark. Slight brown discoloration can occur with minerals in the water, but the contents are still safe for consumption.

- SLIMY, SPONGY, BUBBLING, OR FOUL FOOD—This is disgusting even to the untrained person.

CANNING EQUIPMENT LIST AND TIPS

- CANNING JARS—Glass, free of chips, manufactured by Ball or Kerr in the United States

- TWO-PIECE LIDS—a new metal vacuum lid (must be new with each canning, unless a special multiuse lid) and screw ring

- **BOILING WATER-BATH CANNER**—must be large enough so that water can cover lids by two inches.

- **PRESSURE CANNER**—preferably without a gasket. This is *not* a pressure cooker. We highly recommend the All American Canners for their non-gasketed design. It will be very frustrating and even dangerous if your gasketed canner seal fails.

- **WIRE RACK**—to keep jars off canner floor

- **CANNING FUNNEL**

- **JAR LIFTER AND/OR CANNING TONGS**

- Remember to keep everything absolutely clean when canning.

Root Cellars

There are many types of root cellars. The idea behind this age-old storage process revolves around the desire for a decentralized food-storage location that preserves fresh food. Not all foods can be stored this way; a root cellar is not a refrigerator. The root cellar can be as simple as a temporary cold frame, such as placing hay bales around growing broccoli or lettuce and covering the opening on top with an old storm window. In really frosty weather, an old blanket or another hay bale can be put over the storm window. A root cellar can also be an old refrigerator, buried to utilize the moderate temperature of the earth. If you dwell in cooler parts of the country, an unheated room can make a fine place to store food. Put a thermometer in it and monitor the temperature. Basement root cellars are prominent in New England, and they usually have dirt floors. This allows the space in the root cellar to have a high humidity, which makes for the right condition to store root crops.

A building with a poured concrete floor might be good for storing supplies but it is not a true root cellar. Any metal cans or objects stored inside a root cellar are going to rust because of the humidity. Many people build their cellars into a hillside to use them as a shelter from tornados as well. An under-porch root cellar is a variation of the same concept. Potatoes stored in a root cellar produce the most amazingly delicious

ROOT CELLAR

INSIDE THE ROOT CELLAR

mashed potatoes! Toward the end of the root cellar storage season, as cooler temperatures are harder to maintain, the potatoes start to sprout eyes, many times just in time to plant them for the next season.

One way to extend the season of a root cellar is to crack open the door at night and close it in the morning, trapping in the cool air for the day. The more thermal mass in the cellar, the more insulated the food will be, enhancing the preservation process. Commonly used insulators include soil and leaves. You can also add thermal mass to the tops and side of your root cellar to enhance performance. I am a big fan of an anteroom that acts as a buffer between the outside world and the root cellar. In some locations and soil types, properly installed drains will keep the root cellar from getting too much moisture inside. An added benefit of the root cellar is that it is a great place to hang meat if you are fortunate to be able to harvest a deer or process one of your livestock. Today most meat is just quickly processed and thrown in a freezer without letting it properly age. Knowing when the meat is ready is another lost art that you can learn from dedicated books and individuals.

List of Common Root Cellar Foods

- Apples
- Beets
- Brussels sprouts
- Cabbage
- Carrots
- Celery
- Parsnips
- Potatoes
- Pumpkins
- Winter squash
- Turnips

EXCALIBUR FOOD DEHYDRATOR

Dehydration

Drying is one of the earliest methods of preserving food, dating back to biblical times. When moisture is removed from food, it stops the growth of bacteria, yeast, and mold. Depending on residual moisture, food prepared this way can last six months to two years. Climate is the most important aspect to consider when air or sun drying. When air drying, it is important to bring food in at night so dew does not collect on it. I have heard of using old picture frames with cheesecloth stretched and secured to the wood for drying trays, and have also seen old screens from windows used in the same manner. Galvanized wire can produce an off flavor in the food, so beware before using this process. In either case, the frames need to be braced so air can circulate freely on all sides. Usually after two days of drying, the produce can be turned over. Four days is typical to produce

HOMEMADE
DEHYDRATOR

leathery but pliable produce. Most people will then remove the produce from the frames and freeze it for two to four days or heat on a tray in the oven for ten to fifteen minutes at 175 degrees Fahrenheit to destroy any insect eggs. After that, bring the produce to room temperature and store in airtight jars.

Here in the Deep South of the United States, our food will mold before drying in the sun due to the high humidity of the air. We use an Excalibur Food Dehydrator and have been very pleased with the results. Commercial dehydrators rely on electricity and have trays and a timer. The Excalibur also allows the operator to set the ideal temperature for the product being dried.

I have also made our own dehydrator out of an old refrigerator. I hooked it up to duct work that included a fan and a hot water heat exchanger

> Oxygen absorbers are added to enclosed packaging to help remove or decrease the level of oxygen in the package. They are used to help maintain product safety and extend shelf life.

**ALL AMERICAN
SENIOR FLYWHEEL
CAN SEALER**

run by my wood boiler. I put a thermometer inside the fridge so the temperature could be controlled.

To rehydrate dried produce, cover it with boiling water and let stand several hours to absorb the water. You may choose to use the soaking liquid to cook in.

Dry Pack Canner Sealer

Another method of food preservation that I have come to actually enjoy doing is dry pack using a manual canner sealer. I learned about this when I visited a local Mormon cannery. The trip to the cannery takes a whole day, so I thought it would be nice to be able to can dry goods when I wanted to at home. It has proven to be a great decision, not only for convenience but because the Mormon cannery lacks variety. We have canned so many different foods this way, and when you can buy large amounts of food at great prices this is the way to go. The only drawback is getting the cans and lids for a decent price. I usually buy a pallet or two per year through the Mormon cannery. There are 448 cans per pallet. Don't forget the oxygen absorbers because they remove all the air from the can, minimizing any bacteria growth and aiding in preservation of the food.

Simple Procedure I Use for Dry Canning at Home

1. Buy the bulk food that you want to dry can—rice, beans, macaroni, oatmeal, etc.

2. Pour the food into clean #10 cans.

3. Add an oxygen absorber.

4. Add a lid and take both to the canner sealer.

5. Turn the handle on the sealer twenty-one times to seal the lid to the can.

6. Remove sealed can, label, and store.

Freezing

Unless you live in a frigid region, freezing food will be done in a freezer. A good freezer can be expensive and the ongoing electrical bills add to the expense. Frozen food is superior in texture, color, and flavor to other preserving methods. Airtight packaging reduces evaporation. Pretreating vegetables by blanching yields a better product than those frozen raw. Of course, since preparing for disasters needs careful consideration of any storage that requires ongoing electricity, freezing is only suggested for those who can make enough power to keep their freezer safely below zero. If your freezer is over ten years old, you are wasting a lot of money running it. Look into a new energy-efficient model. You will find they run at half the power consumption. This will give you a better chance of maintaining it with alternative energy sources if the grid goes down for a long period of time.

Curing and Smoking

These are tried-and-true methods for preserving food that have not been explored, yet, by the author. This subject is of great interest to me as I have many ways to produce the smoke, both cold and hot, to preserve food. This topic is another art that seems to be lost in our society. A great book on the subject of smoking and smokehouse design can be found below.

Recommended Further Reading

Austin, Rick. *Secret Garden of Survival; How to Grow a Camouflaged Food Forest.* Self-published, 2012.

Bernstein, Sylvia. *Aquaponic Gardening; A Step-by-Step Guide to Raising Vegetables and Fish Together.* New Society Publishers, 2011.

Bubel, Mike and Nancy. *Root Cellaring: Natural Cold Storage of Fruits & Vegetables.* Storey Publishing, LCC, 1991.

Costenbader, Carol. *The Big Book of Preserving the Harvest: 150 Recipes for Freezing, Canning, Drying and Picking Fruit and Vegetables.* Storey Publishing, LLC, 1997.

Marianski, Stanley, Adam and Robert. *Meat Smoking and Smokehouse Design.* Outskirts Press, Inc., 2007.

Rogers, Marc. *Saving Seeds: The Gardener's Guide to Growing and Storing Vegetable and Flower Seeds.* Storey Publishing, LLC, 1990.

Van Loon, Dirk. *The Family Cow.* Storey Publishing, LLC, 1976.

SHELTER
Should I Stay or Should I Go?

Whether you are bugging out or bugging in, the basics to riding out either a natural or man-made disaster are all the same. Shelter necessities despite your location, bug-out plan, or bugging-in scenario will be the focus of this chapter. Have you considered how you would cook your food in a grid-down situation? How would you keep yourself and your family clean? What methods would you use to stay warm or cool depending on the seasons? What will you do to protect yourself from the worst-case disasters that can strike a shelter: an EMP or a fire? Careful consideration of these issues will not only enable you to keep your family happy and comfortable during a disaster, it could also save your life.

MOUNTAIN RETREAT

SHELTER LOCATION

Factors to Consider When Relocating

A significant number of folks believe that moving to low-population density area is the best solution to prepare for TEOTWAWKI. While there are benefits to relocating to such areas, there are obstacles as well. Before deciding to move away to a region that has been hyped as the best (or only, depending upon the article headline) place to ride out doomsday, you should ask yourself a series of potentially life-saving questions. Would residents of my new area be willing to help out a stranger or steal from a stranger should civil unrest or a reduction of essential resources occur? In all likelihood, even the most generous and Christian families near your new abode would be less likely to offer to share resources or band together with a relative stranger than someone they had seen at church or the grocery store a few thousand times.

Familiarity with an area could be as important as the seemingly foolproof shelter constructed there. While we may want to believe that once we're in our shelter, we are safe and secure, any natural or man-made disaster could prompt our rapid departure at any time. If the marauding hordes often referred to in civil unrest scenarios overrun your property or a wildfire (or perhaps arson) strikes your location, knowing how and where to retreat would assuredly enhance your survival outcome. Preppers who have relocated to an area either in or outside of the United States will be unfamiliar with their new surroundings, the culture, or even the language. You can feel quite isolated. When I moved to my current location it took me many years to know it as well as I knew the area I grew up in.

> The Rule of Threes provides a guideline of how to prioritize basic survival skills: first shelter, then water, and lastly food.
>
> A human can survive for:
>
> - 3 minutes without air
> - 3 hours without a regulated body temperature (shelter)
> - 3 days without water
> - 3 weeks without food

These are but a few of the potential problems associated with following the relocation trend instead of fortifying a shelter in your native area. If you choose to relocate then you and your family should attempt to assimilate into the community as quickly as possible. As mentioned in the previous chapter about food storage, understanding the growing zones and environmental fluctuations involved with growing and raising food is integral to developing a sustainable food source. The crops and livestock that you are the most familiar with may not be feasible in a different region of the country or the world. Practical Preppers advocates a shelter plan that will allow you to stay within your home or in a nearby bug-out location instead of relocating to an area where there are, quite frankly, too many unknowns.

BUYING PROPERTY

If you do choose to relocate or purchase land for a bug-out location, selecting a good property is of the utmost importance. Choosing the right property could be one of the biggest decisions of your life, whether you decide to relocate to a different area of the country or from an urban to a rural locale in the same region. All real estate agents are not created equal. Neither the real estate agent who advertises frequently on billboards nor the one who has found friends a piece of land with a beautiful view to retire upon may be up to the task of finding a bug-out retreat or new bugging-in location.

The cost of the land is perhaps the most insignificant item on the land-purchase checklist. Of course the property must fit comfortably within your budget, but the attributes of both the land and the surrounding community must be the first "deal breaker" topics mentioned when meeting with a real estate agent. The agent should be more than aware of the geographic attributes and topography requirements your bug-out location or new homestead must possess.

Present the agent with a checklist of future land uses before he or she takes you to walk the property. The list could be either generated by you, if you are already experienced at gardening, raising livestock, digging wells, maintaining ponds, as well as solar or wind energy system location needs, or by the requisite professionals if your skill set lacks the abilities needed to determine the land attributes necessary for any of the above purposes. Do not hesitate to arrange for a potential contractor or agricultural professional to accompany you on the land showing.

General Factors to Consider When Buying Property

- Southern exposure
- Water sources
- Land attributes: flat land for growing and pastures, woods for hunting, etc.
- Security issues
- Size (based on the number of people to support)
- Regional concerns

Make sure the land has southern exposure. This will save you a considerable amount of money when it comes to heating your structures and can also allow you to maximize solar production for producing electricity or hot water. Of course, food production is also maximized by having access to the most sunlight possible.

Water sources and water-source location always rank very high when it comes to selecting a property. Now, if water is not obviously flowing or if no springs are bubbling up you can have a well drilled. As was mentioned in chapter 1, the place where you choose to drill can mean the difference between a dry, poor producer, or a highly productive sustainable well. The best situation for a water source is having it placed on a higher elevation so that it can be delivered to your shelter by gravity. The next best alternative is to pump water to an elevated storage tank. This also allows water to be distributed via gravity to your shelter, garden, or livestock.

If you plan on hunting to help put food on the table, you will want a densely wooded area for wildlife to inhabit. Rolling terrain with many hollows and wooded ridges is a prime natural habitat for turkey. Flat and well-drained land is needed for crops of all types and open pasture areas are ideal for a variety of livestock. These are but a few of the land attributes your new location must possess to be successful in your sustainable food supply endeavors. Another area to consider (which we will delve into in more detail in chapter 7) will be security concerns.

Consider what is referred to as "avenues of approach" when it comes to your property. An avenue of approach is a route that can be used by an attacking force. It can be a main highway, driveway, or deer path through the woods. The more avenues of approach, the more attention you will need to pay to watching these areas and potentially blocking them in a crisis situation.

The size of the property needed to "weather the storms" will also heavily depend on the number of people sustained, how productive the soil is, and the amount of fuel sources whether biomass, solar, wind, hydro, etc. Having a property where you use selective harvesting practices and replanting of trees will allow you to have a never-ending fuel source for heating and cooking and possibly even building. When it comes to maximizing space there is a lot to be learned from the permaculture crowd. Permaculture can mean permanent agriculture or permanent culture and is basically a philosophy of working with nature to create a sustainable environment.

Lastly, it is important to consider regional concerns such as weather history, population density, proximity to nuclear reactors, fault lines, and flood plains. You might not be able to filter out all these factors but the safer the location the easier it is to minimize risks.

Building on Your Property

You might find the "perfect" property that meets all of your goals but there are still many things to consider when it comes to the actual location of the shelters you will build or outfit on that property. Watch out for the realtor who tries to sell you "the view." I have consulted on many properties that had vistas to die for but were a nightmare to get water to or to secure.

Factors to Consider When Building

- Ideal elevation for security
- Solar panels: shading, visibility, distance from power storage, orientation to the sun
- Underground rooms
- Sturdy, fireproof materials

From a security standpoint you typically do not want your shelter located on the topographical crest of the land. You would want to choose a lower crest, or what is called the *military crest*. The military crest is an area on the forward or reverse slope of a hill or ridge just below the topographical crest from which maximum observation and direct fire covering the slope down to the base of the hill or ridge can be obtained.

Careful site evaluation for power production will pay dividends. You must evaluate a possible shelter site for solar on a year-round basis.

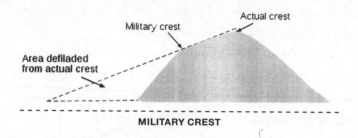

Area defiladed
from actual crest

Military crest

Actual crest

MILITARY CREST

This should take into account shading, panel visibility from avenues of approach, and also how far the power from the panels needs to be run to where it is used to either charge batteries or interface with the grid.

Consider the orientation in regards to the sun's path. Typically, the most economical way to secure solar panels is to mount them to a roof. The mounting system will also add considerable structural strength to your roof. The ideal roof pitch and hence the angle for your solar panels is simply the latitude of your location. This is because your latitude is the same as the angle of the sun in the sky halfway between midwinter and midsummer. In our region of the Southeastern United States the latitude is between 34 and 35 degrees. Typical roof pitches in our areas are 6/12, 8/12, and 12/12. An 8/12 pitch roof is 33.7 degrees off of horizontal and therefore very close to ideal for our area. In summer, the sun will be about 15 degrees higher in the sky, and 15 degrees lower in winter. Tilting your panels at the halfway point maximizes the sun captured year-round. I have found that since solar panel costs have plummeted, adding a few panels to your array is much more cost effective than adding a tracking system.

I hope you are starting to see that picking a property and then building on it can involve many variables that are usually interconnected. A systems approach that includes both passive and active energy production, water delivery systems, and security will get you on the right path to a sustainable shelter. Finding a location that has infrastructure already in place can save you a lot of time and money. The time you will save by having established roads and buildings, water, and power systems cannot be overestimated. We have taken many an existing home and turned it into a sustainable retreat.

The construction techniques for homes vary greatly depending on where they are located in the world, and for the purposes of this book we will only mention a few things to consider when building your shelter. If you can, you want to take advantage of ground temperature for staying cool when it is hot and hot when it is cold. The easiest way to do this is to use the constant temperature of the ground to your advantage. If a good portion of your structure is underground then you will realize these benefits. Of course, locations with a high water table would not be able to have underground structures due to potential flooding.

Building with materials that are fireproof or fire resistant will bring a great peace of mind. Building your structures above and beyond the local codes can also pay off. An example of this would be gluing and screwing the external sheeting on your home. This technique is not required in my area, but homes that have been built this way have stood through hurricanes when neighboring homes were blown away. Diagonal strapping and boxing will also exponentially increase the strength of your home.

OUTFITTING YOUR SHELTER

Whether you are relocating, in process of building, or have decided to stay put, let's discuss what it's going to take to not only survive but thrive in that location. No matter the disaster scenario that we might face in the future, we all want to have the best shot at being able to provide for as many people as possible. If you are not prepared you will be a part of the problem and not the solution.

When it comes to outfitting your shelter with life-sustaining needs I am going to target five areas:

- Power
- Heating

- Cooking
- Hot water
- Sanitation (and morale)

These are the areas that I find most people trying to prepare for disasters have either overlooked or found themselves too overwhelmed to figure out what to do. We have devoted chapter 4 to power sources and power resupply plans for a grid-down scenario. There, we will break each one down into solutions that will start from the easiest and progress to the more complex. When it comes to heating, we recommend a biomass solution but will mention other methods as well. For cooking, we will share simple and effective ways to cook and preserve the food we have stored or plan to harvest. The topic of sanitation will revolve around the ability to produce the most elusive prep and that is hot water.

HEATING

It still gets brutally cold at times in most of the United States. We recently went through a Polar Vortex and many places in the country experienced record cold temperatures and windchills. Cold weather coupled with power outages is a deadly combination. Without electricity, some heating systems do not work, fans do not blow, fuel cannot be pumped, and ignitions do not light. Heat is not only important to regulating your body temperature: If your shelter is without heat for an extended period of time water pipes can freeze and burst. If not caught in time that can also lead to flooding. Having an off-grid backup or primary way to keep your shelter warm is extremely important.

Heaters and Methods to Stay Warm

No matter where you live there are techniques you can use to stay warm using "heat storing" methods. Starting from your body out, this includes layered clothing, high quality sleeping bags, and setting up a room within a room concept. The idea behind this is basically making your living space smaller. You can do this by making walls or partitions within a room. You can stack boxes, books, or furniture and then drape blankets or sheets over them. You are building a room within a room. Use Mylar emergency blankets to keep the heat in. So there are many things you can do before you even begin to need an external heat source to help you store the heat you have.

Heaters

Heaters for crisis situations include kerosene heaters, propane heaters (portable and fixed), and woodstoves. Kerosene heaters are great space heaters that require no external power. Make it a practice to do three things with them. Fill them outside, start them up outside, and, once you bring them in, crack a window for ventilation. As with any open flame devices, they produce carbon monoxide. Propane heaters like the Mr. Heater brand can be used indoors and work great as long as you have enough stored fuel.

Old-School Heating Methods

A primitive method that I believe works great is to heat large pieces of soapstone either on a stove inside or on an outdoor stove and use them as bed warmers. When you are cold it is very hard to get a good night's sleep and you are burning up too many calories to stay warm. Hot water bottles work as well but nothing beats the thermal properties of soapstone. They can also be placed in a room and they will radiate heat for hours. I heat them in our wood cookstove oven and then wrap them in a large towel before placing them in a bed. Be careful not to heat them too much or they will scorch the sheets and blankets. They radiate so much heat that they will run you out of the bed! Soapstone is sometimes used for construction of fireplace surrounds, cladding on metal woodstoves, and as the preferred material for wood-burning masonry heaters because it can absorb, store, and evenly radiate heat due to its high density and magnesite ($MgCO_3$) content. By the way, soapstone can make great ice cubes as well and they won't dilute your sweet tea or whiskey!

You can also heat rocks or bricks if you do not want to pay for soapstone warmers. Many people have saved their lives and the lives of others through the simple process of heating objects and carrying those objects to the place of "heat storing" whether it is a small room or a stranded vehicle.

WOODSTOVES AND WOOD HEATERS

Ahh! There is nothing like the heat from a woodstove on a frigid day! I have seen every type of woodstove known to man and I am a big fan. A woodstove that is correctly installed in your shelter is peace of mind and even more important than water in cold climate. I recommend a stove that makes sense for your climate: soapstone up north, steel down south, and cast iron in the middle. Sometimes you just need to take the chill off and soapstone will just keep putting the heat out when you want to be cooler. A steel stove heats quickly and therefore cools quickly. Cast-iron stoves are similar to steel stoves thermodynamically but can be more ornate. I always tell people to consider buying dual-purpose stoves that do not

PIONEER PRINCESS WOOD COOKSTOVE

have any fans. By dual purpose I mean a stove that not only heats but that you can cook on as well. Many stoves today are jacketed and air is blown around the firebox and exhaust out the front. The surface temperature of the outer jacket is not hot enough to cook with. Instead, get a freestanding stove without an outer jacket, and if the stove is soapstone make sure you can get at least a trivet to cook on. The trivet comes in contact with the top of the firebox so it will reach those 400 °F+ temperatures for you to cook with.

TO BORROW A SAYING FROM THE AMISH

"When you stop to think, a cookstove is one of the most sensible ideas man has ever put fire to—an invention that will cook your meals, provide hot water, bake your bread, roast your turkey, dry your mittens, warm your feet, and heat your home. . . ."

I make it a priority that no matter where I live I will have a wood cookstove. I tell people that if they have a hand pump for their well and a wood cookstove in their shelter then they don't need much else! A wood cookstove should be outfitted with as large as possible firebox, oven, water reservoir, warming closet, and water coil.

WOOD BOILERS

For fifteen years I told friends and family I was researching outdoor wood boilers before I bought one. In reality it took me that long to afford one! An outdoor wood boiler has many advantages and a few disadvantages.

**CLASSIC WOOD
BOILER**

1. SAFETY—The fire is outside away from your shelter.

2. HEALTH—The smoke is kept outdoors.

3. All the wood mess, bugs, and dust are kept outdoors.

4. All the hot water you could ever want.

5. Heat can be evenly distributed throughout your shelter.

6. You can retrofit most existing shelters with one.

DISADVANTAGES:

1. Requires electricity to run the circulating pump and thermostatic controls

2. Produces more smoke than the neighbor might care for

3. Cost

COOKING

When I consult on site and analyze someone's level of preparedness, I typically find that if a person has stored enough food for the timeframe they are preparing, they rarely have a way to prepare, heat, or cook it. Some folks do such a great job making sure they have enough calories per person per day but what about the Btus per meal per day? I have seen a year's supply of food on the shelves and alongside it a few bottles of Coleman fuel and a campstove! When I approach the discrepancy I sometimes get the defensive "I will just cook outside on a campfire."

Knowing the client has never done that for more than one meal a year, I do mention that if all your meals are going to be cooked that way, be prepared for a premature death for the chef! The number two cause of illness in the world behind waterborne diseases is respiratory illnesses due to poor air quality. Mainly it is women and children who are exposed to emissions from cookstoves! Like all preparedness areas, you just do not know what you are capable of doing or producing until you practice.

ALL AMERICAN
SUN OVEN

Make sure you have a safe, reliable grid-down cooking method that you are comfortable using to prepare all your meals day in and day out.

There are so many stoves and widgets available for boiling water and cooking food. I have at least twelve different alternative cookstoves and have put them through their paces. I am neither a chef nor a good cook. I am an engineer who loves to analyze things, make comparisons, and pick the best tool for the job, and when it comes to cooking food in a crisis situation that is my approach.

Sun Oven

A new approach is the solar oven. A box with fold-out reflectors, it captures the energy of the sun and concentrates it on the food. It requires no external power to operate. The disadvantage is repositioning the oven to collect the maximum solar energy. So if you want to roast that chicken, you still end up chasing it around the yard! These work great in places with high solar output, like the Southwest. There are many people who have mastered cooking in these—check out SolarChef1 on YouTube.

Fuel Stoves

There are many inexpensive multiple burner stoves that use propane. They have the advantage of enabling you to cook two or more pots' worth of food at once, but your supply of fuel may be limited. Another advantage is their efficient clean burn. Using one inside of a house is also possible. Coleman makes a whole line of duel fuel stoves that burn gasoline or Coleman fuel. They also have propane stoves. Personally, I am just not a big fan of "cooking on gas." Gasoline within inches of an open flame scares me. These stoves do use very little fuel and produce almost twice as many Btus as propane. Many have oven accessories that can sit on top of the burner.

Backpack Stoves

Tiny and lightweight, I consider these an essential component in your bug-out bag. They can also be used around the shelter for light cooking, such as boiling water for reconstituting meals.

Rocket Stoves

These are sturdy biomass stoves requiring no power to operate. They burn very little fuel and are very clean, reducing carbon monoxide emissions. They can be constructed by stacking bricks in the appropriate configuration or they can be purchased from a variety of manufacturers. To date, my favorite is the SilverFire Survivor. I have put at least a half dozen through their paces for product reviews. The latest and greatest stoves use a primary and secondary combustion to further reduce fuel consumption and CO emissions.

Gasifiers

My favorite biomass stoves are of the TLUD (Top Lit Up Draft) design. They are easy to load with fuel and light, have fewer emissions than rocket stoves, and they burn the least amount of fuel of any biomass stove. We have used these for cooking, grilling, and canning. The only disadvantage

SILVERFIRE
SURVIVOR
ROCKET STOVE

is that forced air is required, so a small amount of power (less than 3 watts) is needed for the fan. More information on gasifiers can be found in chapter 4 (p. 163).

Grills and Smokers

Heavy ceramic grills and smokers like the Big Green Egg are also sustainable biomass cooking solutions. Making your own hardwood charcoal for a grill or smoker is fairly simple: place wood chips in a closed metal container and put it into a fire. Wait until no more gas is expelled

SILVERFIRE
HUNTER GASIFIER

from the edges of the container. Let it cool. While you are cooking one meal, you can prepare your charcoal for the next.

Cookware

Have a variety of cast-iron cookware; I recommend Lodge products. Cast-iron griddles sit nicely on grates. Cast-iron frying pans can be placed directly over fire. Dutch ovens can hang or sit directly over a fire and will bubble away for hours. If you have more people to cook for at your retreat, these may need to be larger than what you now use for your family. One

THE BIG GREEN
EGG

of the nice things about cast iron is it does not show the soot and it can be reconditioned with a wire brush and some steel wool. Once you brush down a pot, you can oil it—I like solid shortening—and reheat it to make a finish. And then you have a new piece of cookware.

Outdoor Kitchens

Outdoor kitchens are great in summer when you don't have air-conditioning and your house is already hot. When the harvest comes in, you need room to can and a way to dissipate the tremendous amount of heat generated while canning. We recommend outfitting a deck or a porch with the stoves mentioned above, and tables to prep, prepare, and preserve your food.

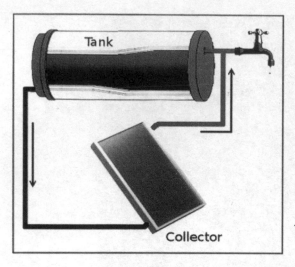

Tank

Collector

HOT WATER

Another area that is often overlooked for shelters is the ability to have hot water in a grid-down scenario. Without hot water at the shelter I am in trouble. I have a wife, four children, a mother-in-law, and a bunch of other people who are looking to me for hot showers and hot water on demand, just like when things are working normally. So how can we keep everybody clean and happy?

Solar Hot Water

TYPES OF SOLAR HEATERS FOR DOMESTIC WATER HEATING

In the simplest terms, solar water heating systems can be either active or passive, but the most common are active systems. Active systems rely on pumps to move the water between the solar heat collector and the storage tank, while passive systems rely on gravity and the principle of thermo siphoning to naturally circulate water as it is heated. Heated water is less dense, lighter, and naturally rises. The cooler water "falls" down, completing the cycle.

Many companies have taken the active systems and started powering the pumps with a small solar panel. This way the system is 100 percent powered by the sun, like a passive system, but has the advantages of much easier installation.

Solar water heating systems sometimes require a back-up system for cloudy days and times of increased demand. Conventional storage water heaters usually provide backup and may already be part of the solar system package. A back-up system may also be part of the solar collector, such as rooftop tanks with thermo siphon systems. Solar systems may also use an on-demand or tankless water heater for backup. We will explain tankless heaters later (p. 98).

I have also seen even simpler designs where a coil of black polyethylene

**PORTABLE SOLAR
SHOWER**

pipe is placed on a roof and is passively heated while water is pumped through the coil. Dangerously hot water can be produced this way as it can only be crudely regulated by the amount of flow through the pipe. Active and passive types of systems can also be further broken down into direct loop and indirect loop, and indirect loop systems have yet another subcategory called drainback systems. There have been many variations and nuances designed into solar hot water heating systems and they are beyond the scope of this book. Two great resources on solar hot water systems are Sunward Systems in Shelburne, Vermont, and SOLARHOT in Raleigh, North Carolina.

Larger solar panels can also be arranged to provide some heating to your home as well. However, the amount of heat provided is generally very small and it is not normally considered cost effective.

There are also portable solar showers that rely on direct heat from the sun to warm the water in a bladder. By keeping the bladder elevated, a person can take a conservative shower.

TANKLESS HEATERS

Tankless or on-demand water heaters use a combination of water pressure, propane, and an igniter to provide instant hot water. The size of the heater can be scaled to meet your needs. I really like the Eccotemp brand for its extensive line of indoor and outdoor units at a reasonable price point. They even have battery operated units. I can ignite mine with two AA batteries. I am hoping to modify one soon to run off of syngas (p. 163) that has been stored in propane tank. This gave me sustainable on-demand hot water!

THERMO SIPHON WOODSTOVES COIL

For every cookstove we sell, we recommend adding a stainless steel water coil to the firebox. The coil runs between the stove and an elevated water tank, and it becomes a heat exchanger, moving heat from the wood fire into the cold water. As the water heats up it rises in the coil to the tank. The colder water in the tank is "siphoned" to the bottom of the tank and into the

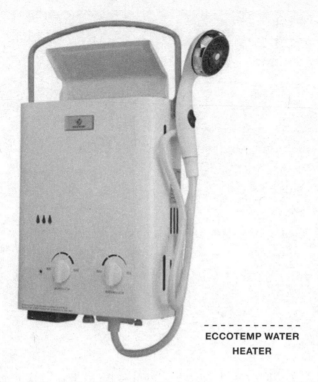

coil. As long as there is heat applied to the coil and the system is full of water, the circulation will begin. This system can be plumbed into the domestic water system. Pressure relief valves must be installed on these systems as high temperatures and pressures can be produced in the coil.

WOOD BOILERS

As I mentioned earlier (p. 89), a wood boiler or biomass boiler is a great way to heat a home and the heat from hot water is one of the most appealing forms of home heater. The boiler's hot water can also of course be used to heat a shelter's domestic hot water through a water to water heat exchanger. We use them on standard water heaters without pumps and again employ the thermo siphon process. To see how much water I could heat with our wood boiler, I decided to heat our 20,000-gallon aboveground swimming pool to 102 degrees Fahrenheit as a surprise to my children one Christmas

NYLE GEYSER

day. They loved it but dad had to cut a lot of wood to make a 20,000-gallon hot tub. It was an exercise in frustration trying to keep it heated to 102 degrees when the outside temperature was 30 degrees. This system also works great for heating a greenhouse, and for supplying the heat for our food dehydrator and clothes dryer.

HEAT PUMP WATER HEATERS

There are several heat pump water heaters on the market today. One that I like is called a Geyser and can be retrofitted to an existing water heater. It runs on 120 volts so it can be run easily off of a solar or alternative energy

SWISS ARMY WATER BAGS

system. I have found this option to be a lot less expensive than a solar hot water heating system.

PORTABLE WATER HEATERS

There are portable propane hot water heaters for the camping market that can come in real handy when there is a disaster. Eccotemp and Zodi make portable hot shower units.

HOT WATER BAGS

A Swiss Army water storage bag can hold 5 gallons of potable water. You can hang it up after it has been in the sun for a while and it makes for a real nice hot water hand-washing station.

RADIATORS

Remember those old cast-iron radiators in old school buildings? They're back! If you are trying to heat your shelter with hot water these cannot be beat. I have used these with my wood boiler to eliminate the need

for secondary pumps and fans to heat a room. Additionally, they also have nonpowered thermostatic radiator valves for controlling room temperature.

SANITATION AND MORALE

Sanitation is a dirty subject and therefore often overlooked. However, if you can imagine what it would be like to go a few days—not to mention weeks or months—without basic personal hygiene, clean clothes, or the ability to properly prepare food, you will quickly see that sanitation plays an important part in your quality of life. Hot water is an essential part of this equation, whether it is for food preparation, personal hygiene, or laundry. Garbage and waste disposal also need addressing.

Food preparation requires spotlessly clean areas, previously prepared with soap, and clean hands for any and all in contact. Do not allow cross-contamination of meat/blood with any foods that might be consumed raw. This usually is done by using multiple cutting boards specially designated for each type of food. My wife color-codes these—as we write this together, it turns out I have been using the wrong colored one for the meat! Not to worry! We have plenty of hot water and soap to wash between uses!

Soap is the backbone of all sanitation. Soap and water alone destroy half of all disease-causing germs when brought into contact. Soap is easy to store, lasts a long time, and is cheap. Personal hygiene is important not only for health but for morale. We are used to being a clean people. When we are dirty—and it doesn't take long—it has a profoundly negative psychological effect on us. It is an immediate way to spot who is not doing well based on their appearance.

Clean clothes also contribute to a sense of well-being and good social function. There are many ways to wash clothes but we are so used to the convenience of a washer/dryer combo. Five-gallon buckets with lids and toilet plungers make a great washing system. One bucket is for washing and one is for rinsing. Plunging times will vary based on how dirty the clothes are. The key to all successful off-grid laundry setups is the wringer! Having a good clothes wringer will remove most of the water from the clothes and then they can be hung on the clothesline. Have you ever tried to hand-wash blue jeans and then dry them? A heavy-duty commercial mop bucket wringer works extremely well for this task. You can also buy the roller-style wringer from Lehman's. If a clothesline is not workable in your apartment then a clothes drying rack can be used. My mother used one all the time in the winter next to the woodstove.

Garbage

The day after Christmas 2013, I went to my local recycling station along with everyone else in the area. The compactor could not keep up with the sheer volume of trash. What would it be like after a month without running transfer trucks?

You need to be able to remove the trash from your living area. Be prepared to handle your own trash by burning or burying what you can. If you are going to burn trash make sure to separate out anything that would create an explosion, such as batteries or aerosol cans. I pre-dug a good-sized hole on my property with my tractor for just this purpose. I am not using it now but if the time comes, then I will be glad I do not have to do it by hand. It is safe with sloped sides so no one will get hurt if they fall down into it.

TRASH ACCUMULATION (KOUNOSU)

Human Waste

If you are fortunate enough to have your own septic system then human waste disposal will be status quo. If you are hooked up to a sewer system that is no longer working, pray you are not located in the lowest area as waste always flows downhill. Your dwelling could become the local septic tank. Only through careful planning can your house be isolated from the system via valves or plugs. More primitive ways to deal with human waste are to use outhouses. Porta Potties can be quickly converted into outhouses and we have even mounted them to a plastic pallet that could be moved to a new location once the hole is filled. When it comes to the actual hole, a combination of lime, dirt, and ash can be used to cover the waste and minimize the smell and the spread of germs.

Feminine products that are disposable can be burned. There are some cotton products sold that are meant to be washed and reused. If nothing is left, cotton shirts can be torn and layered and plastic wrap can be used as a barrier to stop breakthrough. Diapers, while they can be burned, are probably better in the ground, buried. Fecal matter shouldn't be aerosolized.

EMP—THE WORST-CASE DISASTER FOR A HIGH-TECH WORLD

An EMP is an energetic radio wave that can overload electronic circuits causing them to malfunction or to be permanently damaged. An EMP is harmless to people physically, just as radio waves are passing through you right now. But an EMP that destroys electronics in critical infrastructure, airplane, and communication systems can lead to the mass destruction of life.

I tell people that if they are truly prepared for an EMP then they are

---

EMP LINGO

EMP—Electromagnetic Pulse. An EMP has three major components that can be caused by a nuclear detonation or a solar event.

HEMP—High-Altitude EMP. This would likely be caused by a nuclear detonation.

E1—A component of an EMP caused by gamma rays emitted by the nuclear warhead. It is a shock wave that can couple directly into small objects such as computers, transformers, and automobiles, causing them to malfunction. An E1 is too fast to be suppressed by lightning arrestors.

E2—EMP component comparable to lightning.

E3—EMP component that is a waveform that can couple with large objects having at least one dimension of great length. This is the component that can wreak havoc with the grid. E3 currents will build and build and melt down any transformer or device connected to the grid.

CME—CORONAL MASS EJECTION—is caused by a part of the surface of the sun exploding into space. It only produces the E3 effect. The grid is susceptible but in general electronics are not. It would take about a day to reach the earth.

SOLAR FLARE—Flares typically only affect radio communications on earth. They make it to earth in about eight minutes.

---

prepared for anything. There are two approaches to preparing for an EMP. One is to decide to take an 1800s approach to preparedness and be able to sustain yourself and your family through simple means. You will have to go off the grid, use mechanical systems for pumping water, heating, and cooking. It is a romantic notion that I see few people able to accomplish. I do recommend that everyone preparing for an EMP, but still wanting to maintain a "normal" lifestyle, have some of these old-school preps. We sell and install wood cookstoves, hand water pumps, and hand-cranked generators that are all EMP proof. We also recommend obtaining as many hand tools as possible for gardening, construction, sewing, and mechanical work.

Plug and Play: The Faraday Cage

For the majority of people trying to prepare for an EMP, I suggest they take what I like to call a plug and play approach. Determine what you cannot live without and either buy extra or find out what components will fail during an EMP and buy extras of those. Put these extras in what is called a Faraday cage. What I find so ironic is the recommendation I share with folks on how to combat the world's greatest potential threat. I recommend a trash can: a trash can versus a nuclear weapon detonated at high altitude

**HOMEMADE
FARADAY CAGE**

that will wipe out electrical power, transportation, telecommunications, water, and food supply to 317 million people in the United States? Yes, I recommend a trash can but not just any old trash can. It is a $25 galvanized trash can with a tight fitting lid! With this simple prep you can build a Faraday cage that will protect everything inside against an EMP.

Information Overload

I had the privilege of being part of an EMP task force developing an off-grid community that could be a model for others to follow. In the information gathering stage I listened to folks from academia, people trying to get the government to wake up to this threat, and those who work with the military on hardening their equipment to remain operational in the fight. I talked to several companies that test equipment for EMP protection and those that develop ultrahigh speed surge protection. It all boiled down to a few simple facts.

- The average American could never afford the military type solutions I was being presented with.

- If the event was a CME or solar flare the EMP could not couple with and fry anything under three hundred feet in length. I.e., the grid would be susceptible to this type of EMP but my truck would not.

- The most affordable and practical solution would have to be a plug and play Faraday cage approach.

BACK-UP COMPONENTS TO STORE IN YOUR FARADAY CAGE:

- Chainsaw ignition module
- Solar charge controller
- Solar pump controller
- Cell phone
- Dual band radio
- Night vision
- Old laptop
- AM/FM radio
- Voltage regulator for generator
- Alternator for the old truck
- LED flashlight
- Small solar panels

- Nesting (cage in a cage) of Faraday cages greatly increases the level of EMP protection.

So, I built a few nested trash can Faraday cages. I took the outer can and lined it with cardboard since anything you are trying to protect must be insulated from the metal can. I then used Tech Protect Bags to store small components. I also used a smaller galvanized trash can to hold larger objects and placed all these inside the larger cardboard-lined can. I did two simple (not very scientific) tests. I called a cell phone that was in the can and after removing the phone there was no record of a missed call. The other test was to listen for when an AM or FM radio station could no longer be heard on a radio within the can. I believe that a better test would be to take my Faraday cages close to a high-power radio station transmitter and rerun the test.

For further instruction on how to EMP proof your life, consider purchasing our DVD called "Home EMProvements."

Bug-out Vehicle Concerns

Many preppers are concerned about how a potential EMP will impact their vehicle. Depending on the source and therefore the intensity of an electromagnetic pulse, a vehicle may or may not be affected by it. If the source has an E1 component, it is game over for anything that is electronic and not shielded. There are many misleading statements floating around the Internet about which vehicles are EMP proof and which are not. The EMP commission tested thirty-seven vehicles ranging from 1986 to 2002 in an EMP simulation laboratory and found that very few failed and many only had some nuisance failures even up to 25 kV/m. A few cars that were hit with 30 kV/m while they were running, stopped running, coasted to a stop, and then were restarted. Cars that weren't running were not affected by the 30 kV/m EMP. The commission found that cars are a lot tougher against an EMP than most preppers give them credit for. That being said, I am still a fan of having a vehicle with minimal electronics that can be replaced fairly easy. I prefer a pre-90s diesel with mechanical fuel injection, no turbo, and the bare minimum in creature comforts.

Firefighting

When discussing the subject of firefighting with preppers, many times it comes back to having water to put a fire out. Of course fire prevention is so important, but what if your fire department is overwhelmed with calls or just can't make it in time? What can you do? You are now the fire department. As part of the off-grid water systems that I design and install I prefer large lines with at least one "firefighting" station. I run two-inch PVC from an elevated tank to either a threaded or quick-release fire hose connection. At this point water can be directly applied to a fire with a hose, or a portable "trash pump" can pump the water at a much faster rate. As with so many disasters, early detection is key. You cannot wait till your shelter is fully engulfed in flames. On average it takes 30,000 gallons of water to put out a fire like that. But if you hit a small fire early with your stored 2,000 gallons of water, you can save your shelter and minimize the damage.

CAN YOU PREVENT THIS? (KPAHOR)

TRASH PUMP

FIREFIGHTING AND -PREVENTION EQUIPMENT

- **BUCKETS:** Five-gallon buckets are used for everything and this is why you need to have buckets that are never to be touched except for firefighting. A group of people relaying buckets from a water source to a fire can move a lot of water. I have a stack of orange buckets near my pool for just this purpose.

PLASTIC 5-GALLON BUCKET

- **SWIMMING POOL:** My pool has become more of a prepper item than a recreational item. It provides all the water I need to take care of my family for months and it also provides all the water I need or a fire department needs to put out a fire.

- **FIRE EXTINGUISHERS:** Multiple fire extinguishers are recommended. The typical residential grade extinguisher has only about 15–20 seconds of suppression agent inside. I recommend the Cold Fire extinguishers and products for A, B, C, and K class fires. I like having the ability to refill my extinguishers with Cold Fire chemical—and then pressurize them—versus having a bunch of one-shot wonders. You can also use air from an inflated tire to pressurize these extinguishers.

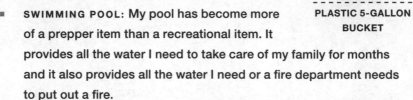

- **SMOKE HOODS:** More people die from smoke inhalation than from actually being burned from a fire. A smoke hood might give you and your family the time necessary to escape from a building or wildfire.

KEEP ONE ON HAND

- **INDIAN BACKPACK:** These portable 5-gallon firefighting pumps are not cheap to purchase. They have a short hose and a pump that will put out a strong stream of water for twenty feet or so. They are designed to be carried on your back and to suppress small fires.

- **BAKING SODA:** The soda smothers the flames from a grease fire before it can spread.

- **CHIMFEX:** The commercial chimney fire extinguisher and an ABC extinguisher can help save your bug-in dwelling should a fire start inside the home.

- **BUNKER GEAR:** Different firefighter suits are used when fighting brush or woodland fires or typical building fires. These are expensive, but used ones can often be found on eBay, or perhaps from local fire departments that are upgrading their gear.

FIRE PREPAREDNESS EDUCATION

You do not have to plan on becoming either a professional or volunteer firefighter in order to sign up for the basic forty-hour class. Ask local firefighters about training sessions and community college courses so you can learn how to use firefighting hand tools, dig firebreaks, and other life-saving tips now, before the power grid goes down and a popping and cracking transformer destroys your barn, livestock, garden, and home.

FIRE PREVENTION

- Choose to build your shelters with fireproof materials such as concrete blocks and metal roofs.

- Place battery-powered fire detectors everywhere and test them regularly.

- Make sure your structures are clear (on the outside) of leaves and debris.

- Have fire escape ladders for the second and third floors.

SMOKE DETECTOR

CONCLUSION

As you can tell from this chapter on shelter, there are many things you can do to prepare before a crisis occurs. I hope that it has motivated you to start on at least one or two projects that could really enable you to either weather a storm or be able to provide shelter to someone less fortunate.

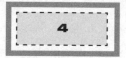

POWER

Lights Out!

A Little Bit of Electricity goes a long way.

—Scott Hunt

We are an electricity- and fuel-dependent society. We see this every time there is a natural disaster. When critical infrastructure such as municipal water systems, electrical power, cell towers, and fuel delivery are interrupted, it does not take long for the effects on life to be revealed. Developing your own back-up power systems can be a daunting task. As in previous chapters, I will start with storage then proceed to a resupply plan. Having fuel on hand for your vehicles, generators, and stoves can give you as much peace of mind as having food on your shelves.

POWER STORAGE: FUEL

Fuels can be considered the foundation for power production and they are analogous to the previous chapter's storage sections. We will now delve into fuel storage and types of fuel. It would be nice to be able to afford and store as much fuel as you would like but fuel storage can be problematic. There are a few important things to consider up front before storing various fuel sources:

1. Fire safety

2. Local codes for how much and what methods are allowed

3. Security concerns whether they be fire, or the sight and smells of the fuel that give away your location

Propane

Propane can be a great choice for fuel storage for the following reasons:

- It can be stored indefinitely.

- It has a high Btu rating.

- It burns clean and leaves engines cleaner than other fuel types.

- It has been one of the fuels of choice to complement alternative energy sources such as solar and wind.

I have a 1970 propane generator whose inner workings look as they did the day it rolled off the assembly line. Many have chosen propane for the variety of preparedness solutions it offers. A list of propane devices and appliances that I see used are:

- Generators
- Refrigerators
- Freezers
- Lighting

- Water heaters
- Ranges/ovens
- Clothes dryers

When it comes to a propane install, I prefer buried tanks to aboveground simply because they are safe and secure that way. However, purchasing tanks to bury in the ground can be very expensive. We recommend leasing the tanks on a yearly basis. Who is going to come pull the tank out of the ground during a crisis time? If you go with aboveground tanks I recommend setting them far from your buildings and also fencing them in for security and fire protection. Propane can be such a welcome fuel source when the grid is down that you might not feel that you can just reach over and turn a knob and have the stove light up or have the water piping hot. I tell folks to consider their propane storage like money in the bank and to use other means such as wood or solar to keep that propane in "savings."

> The British thermal unit (Btu) is the amount of energy needed to cool or heat one pound of water by one degree Fahrenheit. The Btu unit is most often used as a measure of power (as Btu/h).

Gasoline

Gasoline storage for short-term situations is smart for a couple of reasons:

- It's easy to use in vehicles, generators, and chainsaws.
- It will always be in high demand when the power goes out.

Whether you need to bug out or you need to clear out the debris left from a storm, you should keep gasoline on hand. I have found that you can store gasoline for about two years but the quality begins to degrade immediately.

PRI-G GASOLINE TREATMENT

There are additives like Pri-G that can slow the fuel from breaking down. I prefer to store this fuel in a shed or building not attached to my home as it is, of course, highly flammable. I always recommend buying and storing the highest octane nonethanol gasoline I can find. But that can be hard to find for most folks.

The Energy Independence and Security Act of 2007 mandates that 15 billion gallons of corn ethanol be blended into the nation's gasoline supply by 2015. Since ethanol started to be added to our gasoline supply I have noticed more and more problems with my small-engine equipment. Alcohol is corrosive and can degrade plastic, rubber, or even metal parts in the fuel system that weren't engineered to use alcohol-bearing fuel. As a solvent, ethanol frees up the gunk in fuel tanks and engines, which can then clog carburetors and fuel lines. The size of a small engine exaggerates this effect, as smaller fuel lines and smaller components are more quickly compromised by these deposits. I have replaced more fuel lines and carburetors on this equipment than ever before. Remember, too, that alcohol tends to absorb and hold water. Sometimes, if conditions are just right, all the water and alcohol in your fuel settle out in the bottom of the tank, and when the fuel pickup is only accessing this water alcohol mixture, the engine is not going to start.

I had to stop purchasing gasoline from a station close to my home in favor of a nonethanol supply on the other side of town. Bottom line, don't waste your time and money trying to store gasoline that is now 10 percent and heading for 15 percent or higher alcohol content. If you find yourself having to use this new fuel on older engines or small engines then I recommend you run them dry if you are not going to use them for a while. How times have changed. The recommendation for gasoline used to be always keep a full tank.

Diesel

My favorite fuel for preparedness is diesel due to its many advantages:

- Diesel engines are more fuel efficient than gas.
- It's not as flammable as other fuels like gasoline.

- **It stores much longer than gasoline.**
- **There are many fluids that can be substituted for diesel, such as vegetable oil.**

When it comes to getting work done it is hard to beat diesel. Just check with the train company CSX. In 2009, CSX trains averaged 468 miles per gallon of diesel per ton. One gallon of diesel is equivalent to roughly five-hundred-man-hours of labor. With a diesel engine tractor, in one hour I can plow and till one acre of garden, having it fully prepared for planting. I still don't think that five hundred men could prepare that much soil in one hour of backbreaking work.

I have stored diesel fuel for up to ten years and then run it without a problem in my generators. That was prior to 2007. Yes, like gasoline, diesel chemistry was also changed that year to what is called ULSD (Ultra-Low-Sulfur Diesel). The jury is still out on the effects of this change. Companies like BP tell us that when low sulfur diesel fuel is stored underground, it can be expected to last at least five years provided steps are taken to keep water and fungus out—and potentially up to ten years or more with regular inspection.

Keep Water Out of Your Fuel!

It is the number one killer! Water is the essential element that microbes need to establish themselves and multiply, because they live in the water-diesel interface. A tank that has little water in it is at less risk for developing this situation. The problem is that once the microbes are in the tank, they produce acids that wreck fuel quality and corrode tanks; they clog filters and they continue to reproduce until you put out extra money to get rid of them by using a biocide. You can also add a water absorbing filter to your system but of course you need to stock enough filters to handle the amount of fuel you plan on stocking. For long-term storage, PRI-D stabilizes

PRI-D DIESEL
TREATMENT

FUEL STORAGE PLAN

fuel so completely that algae and slime do not form. We believe that long term, this is a more effective process than the use of biocides. However, for diesel consumers who want a quick, effective algae kill, PRI manufactures PRI-OCIDE, an EPA-registered diesel fuel microbiocide.

When it comes to fuel storage, I recommend keeping your fuel tanks full, cool, and protected from the elements. Water can be introduced into a tank that sits in the open and day in and day out is subjected to large temperature fluctuations. This temperature differential can introduce condensate inside the tank. A full tank greatly helps but sometimes your tank cannot be always kept full if you are using and rotating the supply. I like storing diesel in an elevated tank as it is the easiest way to drain off the water that might enter the tank, as water settles on the bottom. Slightly angle your tanks toward the water drain. If you do not control the water issue and you live in a northern climate, it will wreak havoc once the watery fuel is introduced to the engine as it will freeze.

One of the biggest advantages of diesel is that diesel engines can offer you other alternative fuel options. I have an old two-cylinder diesel engine that has been my experimental fuels engine for the last ten years. I have run this engine on ten-year-old diesel, veggie fuel, biodegradable charcoal fluid, transmission oil, motor oil, and have mixed these different fuel types in varied ratios with great success. Remember, newer engines are not as forgiving as older ones when it comes to varied fuel types and fuel conditions.

Kerosene

Kerosene is a very practical fuel to store. There are several reasons for this:

- **It's versatile—it can be used for heating, lighting, and cooking.**
- **It's an oil, not a volatile fuel, so it is much safer to store. It is not explosive.**
- **It can be stored for many years without significant degradation.**
- **It's readily available and can be purchased in volume at reasonable prices.**
- **It's a dense store of energy—1 gallon contains about 135,000 Btus of energy (almost 50 percent more than a gallon of propane).**

In North America, gas stations offer two types of diesel fuel—according to ASTM D975 these are named No. 1 and No. 2 fuel. No. 1 fuel (kerosene) is more expensive than No. 2 fuel (diesel). Adding No. 1 fuel will lower the point at which the fuel will still flow through the filter. Knowing this can come in handy when unexpected arctic air settles into an area long enough for fuels to start gelling. I have had my tractor simply not run because the fuel gelled due to the cold. When animals are expecting to be fed and the tractors won't run, you have a problem. If you pretreat the tank with a little kerosene, the fuel mixture flows. The fuel filter is typically the first point to become clogged when the fuel gets cold. Adding 10 percent kerosene to diesel will lower the CFPP (cold filter clogging point) temperature by about 5 degrees.

In regions with a cold climate, the standard diesel fuel at fuel stations is required to meet certain CFPP characteristics. Gas stations in colder climates offer "winter ready diesel" for sale to the motorist—there are two ways to achieve this:

- **WINTER BLEND**—The gas station has blended the No. 2 diesel with No. 1 (kerosene) by some percentage.
- **WINTERIZED DIESEL**—The No. 2 diesel has been treated with additives by the diesel supplier.

As the treatment with additives is a cheaper way to enhance No. 2 fuel in winter, most stations offer winterized diesel in cold weather conditions. However, in regions with colder weather, most gas stations offer No. 1 fuel at the same pump, allowing drivers to decide for themselves on a winter blend. Be careful not to add too much kerosene as its lubricity is not as good as No. 2 diesel fuel.

Wood

As one of the oldest forms of fuel in civilization, wood has many advantages:

- Plentiful in areas with dense forests
- Inexpensive
- Renewable using good forest management
- Safe to store

When I was growing up in Upstate New York my middle name was "get wood." Everyone in our family burned wood so no matter whom I was visiting—dad, mom, grandparents—there was always wood to be cut, split, stacked, and loaded into some type of stove. I grew up eating food cooked on a wood cookstove and it is still a fond childhood memory. A sleepover at Grandma's wasn't complete without pancakes cooked on a cast-iron griddle that replaced the top two "eyes" on her stove. Those pancakes, with the neighbor's homemade maple syrup, were to die for. I have never been able to duplicate what was produced on that stove!

The stoves I grew up with ranged from big homemade wood boilers in a basement, to ornate wood cookstoves in the kitchen, to freestanding soapstone stoves in the living room. Where I grew up wood was plentiful and harvesting it rarely put a dent in the supply as the forests delivered quality fuel wood year after year. With best management practices, most forests easily deliver relatively inexpensive fuel every year—between half and one cord per acre—while at the same time being improved to encourage the growth of high-quality tree species, hold back the spread of invasive species, create optimal wildlife habitats, and decrease the likelihood of forest fires.

Responsible use of wood to heat buildings reduces our reliance on imported fossil fuels while strengthening our local economies. It also cuts down on transportation of fuels, which carries costs to our environment as well as to our roads and bridges.

When I set out to prepare for whatever came down the pike I set a goal that I would maximize two abundant resources on my property, water and wood. I knew that if these two resources were managed properly that I would have a well-grounded preparedness plan. I started to look at wood differently than my parents and grandparents had. In researching the uses of wood in the late 1800s and early 1900s I found some pretty fascinating concepts. I found out that not only could I heat my home and cook with wood but that I could also use wood to power engines, make electricity, and power my old truck! As an engineer I was "stoked." Pardon the woodstove expression. If I could heat our home, cook our food, dehydrate our produce, dry our clothes, drive our vehicles, make our hot water, and generate our own electricity then I could get really close to not only being self-sufficient, but could weather any storm that came my way. Not only could I pursue energy independence in the burning of wood, but I could also use the wood for construction purposes.

Before I get into all the different "venues" for wood let me say a word or two about the types of wood and their potential thermal value. What wood species gives off the most heat? You will get the best results and more heat per wood volume when burning the highest density (heaviest) wood you can find. Dense firewood will produce the highest recoverable Btus but all wood must be "seasoned." Seasoning lowers the moisture content and less energy is used to drive off water, which limits heat efficiency. To season or dry your wood properly it is imperative that you build a woodshed to protect the wood from precipitation.

Trees considered to be deciduous (lose their leaves in winter) and more specifically hard hardwoods tend to be a more dense wood and will burn hotter and longer than trees considered to be evergreen or softwood (there are some exceptions). Firewood also tends to burn hotter when seasoned to reduce moisture. Wood heat value is also measured in Btus. The higher the value, the more heat you get per unit of wood. Here is a list of tree species ranked by their heating abilities:

FIVE BEST-BURNING SPECIES

- HICKORY—25–28 million Btus/cord—density 37–58 lbs./cu.ft.

- OAK—24–28 million Btus/cord—density 37–58 lbs./cu.ft.

- BLACK LOCUST—27 million Btus/cord—density 43 lbs./cu.ft.

- BEECH—24–27 million Btus/cord—density 32–56 lbs./cu.ft.

- WHITE ASH—24 million Btus/cord—density 43 lbs./cu.ft.

FIVE POOR-PERFORMING SPECIES

- WHITE PINE—15 million Btus/cord—density 22–31 lbs./cu.ft.

- COTTONWOOD/WILLOW—16 million Btus/cord—density 24–37 lbs./cu.ft.

- BASSWOOD—14 million Btus/cord—density 20–37 lbs./cu.ft.

- ASPEN—15 million Btus/cord—density 26 lbs./cu.ft.

- YELLOW POPLAR—18 million Btus/cord—density 22–31 lbs./cu.ft.

I must also mention a thing or two about safety when it comes to wood.

SPLITTING MAUL

With just about everyone in my family burning wood, I learned a thing or two about cutting and splitting wood at an early age. My stepfather and his family were full-tree loggers during the winter months and I put in the hours limbing and cutting tops from the trees they skidded to the landing. I cut the tops and limbs into firewood lengths while the trees were bucked and loaded for the mill. Learning early on how to run and maintain a chainsaw has really come in handy. Chainsaw manufacturers such as Husqvarna and Stihl have really good tutorial videos on chainsaw operation and maintenance. I also learned how to split wood with a maul and to this day that is how I do it. A maul is a heavy-headed long-handled ax. The head has a sledgehammer shape on one side and an ax wedge on the other.

I always get a kick out of greenhorns who come to my place and try to split wood. There is a technique you learn over time that works best for you and allows you to transfer the most power into the wood. Power, along with accuracy, comes with experience and is required for those downright ornery hard-to-split pieces. For hardwoods, the best maul for the job is an eight-pound maul with a fiberglass handle. The geometry of the maul head comes into play as well. Too narrow, like an ax, and the maul gets stuck. Too wide a taper and there will not be enough penetration to cause the downward forces to split the wood. A prepper's motto should be "right tool for the job." Splitting wood is great exercise but be careful to use consistent form and a good stance. The last thing you want to do is to get hit with the head of a splitting maul.

Another trick my grandfather taught me was to split the tree the way it grows, in other words from the bottom up. This doesn't always work, but it at least reminds me that when that difficult piece of firewood won't yield to the maul, to turn it over and attack it from the other side. We are usually tempted to split the large pieces in half and then the halves in quarters and quarters into eights. But sometimes you can wear yourself out with that approach. On a really tough piece I will work the edges, taking what I can, and I find that this weakens the entire piece. Of course you can "cheat" and buy a wood splitter, but what fun is that?

WOODSTOVES

When it comes to burning wood make sure you understand how the stove you are using should be installed and operated. Follow the building and fire codes in your area, otherwise the insurance company will have no mercy if you have a chimney or house fire. There is nothing scarier than your house being on fire with you and your loved ones inside. I have experienced this and I will never forget the pandemonium that resulted from a chimney fire that turned into a house fire.

Make sure you burn only good quality wood in your stoves. Do not burn household trash! The number of toxic chemicals these materials release into the air when burned could land you in the hospital. They include:

- Dioxins
- Volatile organic compounds (VOCs) (such as benzene, toluene, and methyl chloroform)

GENERAL STEPS TO MAKE, MAINTAIN, AND END A FIRE (ANY FIRE, ANY METHOD):

- **Choose and prepare a location for the fire.**
- **Gather fuel.**
- **Pile some of the fuel in an appropriate manner where the fire is to be situated, ready to be lit.**
- **Ignite some material, usually tinder. This is usually the most difficult (and critical) step.**
- **If necessary, depending on the fire-starting method, blow the tinder into a small flame.**
- **Transfer the flame from the tinder to the actual fire.**
- **Build up the fire by adding fuel.**
- **Maintain the fire as needed.**
- **Put out the fire.**

- Furans
- Halogenated hydrocarbons
- Chlorinated fluorocarbons
- Carbon monoxide
- Carbon dioxide
- Sulfur dioxide
- Heavy metals (including lead, barium, chromium, cadmium, arsenic, and mercury)

Your stove should be able to burn wood as cleanly as possible. If you see smoke, you're not getting the most heat value from your wood, creosote is likely condensing in your stovepipes, and you and your neighbors are breathing potentially toxic pollutants. Moisture is usually the number one culprit when it comes to smoke and incomplete combustion is the second factor. The design of woodstoves has improved leaps and bounds in the last decade or so due to strict EPA regulations. This has brought awareness to those who have burned wood all their lives that there is a better way to burn.

Stoves outfitted with high-tech multiport combustion air injection systems create secondary combustion zones that give a more complete burn. Two- and three-stage gasification stoves have made it possible to pass the most stringent of EPA clean air regulations. Rocket mass heaters have also provided for a cleaner and safer wood-burning experience. The added benefit to the home owner is that these modern stoves burn a lot less wood than the traditional inefficient stove. The difficulty for those preparing is that these new stoves can be very expensive. Not only that, they contain a lot of electronic circuitry that would be susceptible to failure due to lightning strikes or EMP events. There is a lot to be said for having an old woodstove with no fans, no transformers, or fancy electronic controls.

ENERGY RESUPPLY

"Make hay while the sun shines."

Now that we have covered a variety of fuels that you can store for troubled times, let's talk about how they can be used to produce life-sustaining energy if the grid is down for an extended period of time. We will start with human-powered devices and work our way up to larger hybrid systems that use a variety of ways to produce electricity. A little electricity goes a long way!

Small Generators

We are so accustomed to living in a world surrounded by devices and appliances that run off of electricity. When the grid goes down for any reason our level of dependence really begins to reveal itself. The idea that your iPhone could no longer be charged or that cell towers are down causes anxiety in people young and old these days. The ability to communicate requires electricity, whether it is for your cell phone or your

PRACTICAL PREPPERS CRANK-A-WATT

ham radio station. I like to have many ways to make power and one that most everyone, urban or rural, can use is a hand-cranked generator.

Advantages to Hand-Cranked Generators:

- They are virtually silent.
- They can be used to run many critical medical devices like nebulizers for asthmatics.
- They are a good solution for an urban prepper who cannot use solar- or gasoline-powered generators.
- They easily produce usable power at low rpms so that even children can turn them.
- They can be used to charge larger batteries for use elsewhere in the home or shelter.
- They can be adapted to be powered by a bicycle, making it easier to sustain charging power.

Disadvantages to a Hand-Cranked Generator:

1. The sustainable power output is only about 150 watts per hour (an Olympic Athlete can generate 200 watts per hour).

2. The battery needs to be maintained by a battery tender or solar charger.

LIST OF ITEMS SUITABLE TO BE RUN OFF OF A HUMAN-POWERED GENERATOR:

1. Small batteries for flashlights, radios, security devices like night vision

2. Medical devices such as nebulizers and possible CPAP machines

3. Charging larger batteries for ham radio stations

4. RV water pumps

5. Cell phone chargers

6. Laptops and tablets

7. Cordless tool chargers

HAND-OPERATED RADIO
(MORN)

There are also many small hand-operated devices such as flashlights and radios that have built-in dynamos so that they can also be human powered. There are many cell phone hand-crank chargers these days that produce a regulated voltage and many of them have built-in LED lights. They could be the perfect solution to be able to stay in touch with loved ones when you find yourself away from home and without grid power.

Thermoelectric Generators (TEGs)

Another area of "small" power generation that is relatively unknown is sometimes called *energy harvesting*. It is simply using a heat differential to produce a DC voltage. The most practical application of this is sometimes seen in fans that sit on top of woodstoves. A thermoelectric generator in

ECO FAN WITH THERMOELECTRIC
GENERATOR

the fan base receives heat directly from the stove and converts that heat
into electricity. This generator's subsystem consists of no moving parts
and has a reputation of being highly reliable.

A variety of TEGs can be found in various pieces of equipment used
in space. The Apollo astronauts relied on these devices during their moon
missions, and the Cassini and Voyager spacecrafts are also powered by on-board RTGs (radioisotope thermoelectric generators), which work by converting the heat released by the decay of a radioactive source, such as strontium-90 or plutonium-238, into an electric current. In space, the required "cold side" for the device is also easy to supply given that the average temperature is just three degrees above absolute zero ($-273.15\ ^\circ$C), the temperature at which atoms completely cease all motion.

> TEGs depend upon a temperature difference to "drive" the device—so one side needs to be hot and the other side cold. This temperature difference makes the electrons on the "hot" side vibrate more vigorously so they tend to move toward the colder side where the electrons are moving more slowly. This movement gives rise to a current that can be tapped off as electricity.

THE POWERPOT

Back on earth, many automotive companies are working on capturing waste heat from exhaust systems to potentially replace alternators for charging batteries. When it comes to being prepared I want to utilize every technology available to make electricity. TEGs have made their way to the prepper market as either part of a gasification stove or as an accessory that can take heat and charge a cell phone. The PowerPot is one such device. The colder the climate the better these devices work as cold air or water makes for a larger temperature differential and this improves the efficiency of the TEG.

Large Generators

I approach a power system for a shelter from opposite ends. On one end you have the electrical loads you desire to run and the other end is the available power inputs and available budget to go along with it. These types of systems are very difficult to scale so you do not want to have to do it over. The usual struggle is between buying a generator that will get exceptional fuel economy and one that will run everything you would like in your shelter.

Generators use gasoline, diesel, natural gas, or propane. Here are the advantages of each fuel type:

GASOLINE

- Most common fuel source and is easily obtained; has short shelf life
- Increases portability of smaller generators

PROPANE

- Long shelf life
- Clean burning
- Easily stored in both large tanks or smaller 5–10-gallon cylinders
- Obtainable during power outages
- Home delivery available for large tanks

NATURAL GAS

- Unlimited fuel source, no refilling required
- Clean burning
- Available during power outages

DIESEL

- Least flammable fuel source
- Easily obtained
- Fuel delivery available
- Alternative fuels such as biodiesel, waste motor oil, transmission fluid, etc., can be run in some diesel generators.

Fuel-Powered Generators

Earlier in this chapter, we discussed the various types of fuels and how to store them; now, we need to mention the pros and cons of the different types of generators that use these fuels. People tend not to talk about generators much until there is an event like a large hurricane. Then there is a run on all the big box stores and generators are sold out as fast as any other emergency supply. During the event, many people get hurt or hurt others by improperly using them. When it comes to generators, some time and effort needs to be put into determining the right type of generator for the right job.

QUESTIONS YOU SHOULD ASK BEFORE YOU BUY A GENERATOR

- What is the generator's wattage capacity and will it support your needs, including start-up surge power required by some equipment?
- Does the generator have enough outlets to plug in all of the items you want to power?
- How noisy is the generator? Are there noise restrictions in your neighborhood?
- What type of fuel does it use?
- How large is the fuel tank and how many hours of operation will it provide?
- Is the generator easy to move around? Does it have built-in wheels and handles for portability?
- What accessories will I need to run the generator (fuel, heavy-duty extension cords, transfer switch)?

Disposables/Portables

This is what I call the "no name" generators that get purchased up by the thousands when there is a storm. They are made abroad and have generic names such as Champion or Diamond. They are usually very loud little portable units ranging from 1,000 watts to 10,000 watts. They are very handy when you are in a bind and need to keep a few critical appliances running.

> Generator power is measured in watts. Amps X Volts = Watts

For these types of generators, it's important to get the right-size power cord for your generator.

PORTABLE GENERATOR

SELECTING A GENERATOR POWER CORD IS SIMPLE IF YOU FOLLOW TWO STEPS:

1. SELECT AMPS

Portable generators are measured by watts. Power cords are measured in amps. Basically, the larger the amount of amps, the more electricity the cord can handle. For example, a 50-amp power cord is a lot thicker than a 20-amp power cord, allowing it to handle larger wattages. You simply select a power cord that matches the *most powerful outlet* on your generator. If you have a 50-amp outlet, you'll need a 50-amp power cord. If you have a 20-amp outlet, you'll need a 20-amp cord.

2. SELECT SHAPE

The plugs and connectors are purposely designed in different shapes, helping to prevent an electrical overload. If you have a 30-amp or 50-amp

SAFETY TIPS FOR USING GENERATORS:

- Plug appliances directly into the generator.

- Do not attempt to connect the generator directly to your home's circuits or wiring. Have an electrician install a transfer switch and plug the generator into this switch. This will keep the generator from feeding power back into the lines, which could put power company crews working on the lines at risk. This will also protect your generator and home wiring from damage when power is restored.

- Use heavy-duty extension cords from the generator, as overloaded cords can cause fires and equipment damage. Make sure cords are placed to avoid tripping hazards, but don't put them underneath carpets where heat may build up.

- Never run a generator indoors and make sure there is proper ventilation around the unit.

- Never add fuel while the generator is running. Avoid spilling fuel on hot components and put out all flames or cigarettes when handling fuel.

- Consider tri-fuel generators to avoid multiple trips to the gas station and downtime.

- Always have a fully charged, approved fire extinguisher near the generator.

- Don't overload the generator. Use only when necessary to power essential equipment.

- Be cautious handling electrical cords in wet conditions.

outlet, pay special attention to its shape and match the plug on your cord to it.

If you decide you want to be able to run multiple appliances at once, then the best thing to do is hire an electrician and have either a manual or automatic transfer switch installed near your service entrance. A transfer switch is an electrical safety device that makes sure that the circuits that you plan on running with your generator can be isolated to either the electrical grid *or* the generator. If this is not done correctly, the poor electrical lineman who is risking his life to restore your power after a disaster can be electrocuted by your improperly installed generator backfeeding onto the grid. Like generators and power cords, transfer switches come in a full range of power ratings. Make sure the transfer switch is rated high enough to handle the electrical loads that will be running off the generator(s) at any one time.

The Internet is full of wattage calculators and charts on what various appliances, pumps, and motors require. Always err on the side of a larger generator or be prepared to manage your circuit when an outage occurs. One advantage of going with a smaller generator is increased fuel economy. Many whole-house systems are convenient but they do use a lot of fuel.

The biggest problem that you will have with these generators is that after they sit for a year, if you didn't follow the guidelines for gasoline storage (p. 117) they

**FLUKE POWER
METER**

might not start. These are small engines that do not do well with ethanol fuel sitting in them for long periods of time. I have found that turning off the fuel shutoff and then running it until it shuts off has given the best results for being able to restart the generator when I need it.

If getting water out of your well with a generator is one of your objectives, make sure you size the generator correctly. You need to size a generator based on matching the surge rating needed for starting the well pump rather than the power needed to run the pump. Be warned that not having the needed surge capacity on hand can damage the pump motor. Every well setup is different and when a well pump starts up, it already has a load on it from the head pressure of water above it. You or an electrician should take a good quality clamp meter and measure the start-up amps and the run time amps. Remember, generator power is measured in watts: Amps X Volts = Watts. The voltage for residential homes in North America is 120 or 240 volts depending on the appliance.

So your coffeepot that uses 10 amps is using 10×120 volts $= 1,200$ watts/hr. Your clothes dryer running on 240 volts uses 20 amps equaling 4800 watts/ hr. All appliances have power specification labels or tags that tell you what wattage and voltage they require.

When running the well pump off of a generator, always start the generator before the pump motor is started and always stop the motor before the generator is shut down. The motor thrust bearing may be damaged if the generator is allowed to coast down with the motor running. This same condition occurs when the generator runs out of fuel.

Residential Standby Systems

An emergency home standby generator system can automatically restore power to your house in about twenty seconds. When the power goes out, the generator automatically starts and continues to run until power is restored. You can choose a generator that delivers enough power for the entire house (including air-conditioning) or go with a smaller unit and power a few selected circuits, such as the refrigerator, sump pump, furnace fan, and several lights for basic survival.

These all-weather generators are installed outside the home and are wired through an automatic transfer switch to the main electrical panel. The use of an automatic transfer switch is often required when generators are connected to home wiring.

Home standby systems can be fueled by natural gas, propane, or diesel fuel. Many models can be connected to the home's natural gas line, eliminating the need to fill fuel tanks. Standby system capacities range from 6,000 watts up to 40,000 watts and more, and start automatically— even if you are not home.

If you choose propane or natural gas (if available in your area) for your generator then you have, for the most part, eliminated the hassle of worrying about fuel quality, additives, and storage conditions. The majority of propane-fueled standing generators run at the higher of two standardized rpms (1800 and 3600). My personal choice is always a slower runner as it is typically a longer runner and it is quieter. Sound or noise

MY DIESEL GENERATOR

discipline will be addressed in more detail in the security chapter.

I am a fan of diesel generators that run at 1800 rpms because they typically have the longest service life. They also allow you more fuel options as we discussed (p. 119).

Overall, generators are great tools to weather a storm. My personal setup has provided clean electricity for over 1,600 hours or over two months' worth of 24/7 power. During one ice storm I ran my diesel generator for seven days straight. It is a 2-cylinder diesel running at 1800 rpms. I find that a 2–3 cylinder 12,000-watt diesel generator strikes a good balance between having plenty of power and great fuel economy. I run twenty-four hours on eight gallons of diesel. Many residential standby systems use about 1.5 gallons per hour, or thirty-six gallons a day. That is quite a difference. You need to plan your expected time of usage and your storage accordingly. Make sure you can easily start and stop your generator. This allows you to run it only when necessary and greatly conserves your fuel supply.

Batteries

Batteries are energy-storage devices and instead of talking about them in the fuel-storage section I wanted them sandwiched between generators and photovoltaic (or solar) systems as they are the two most widely used methods for charging batteries in a grid-down situation. The batteries I will mention start with the small 50-cent coin batteries and will progress to a $40,000 Ni-FE 48 volt off-grid battery bank that will last a lifetime.

Stocking up on batteries is a must. Once you start practicing using your preparations you start to realize how many batteries you need. Batteries and battery-operated devices allow you to have effective defensive measures. There are many combat or force multipliers that rely on battery power. Without them you will need a lot more manpower and thus a lot more food and supplies to take care of them. I always say that it is a lot cheaper to feed those Dakota Alerts batteries than five to ten grown men sitting out on the perimeter.

Make it a priority to standardize your equipment as much as possible to minimize the different types of batteries you need. For our retreat, AA and CR123s are the mainstays. They are used in radios, alarms, transmitters, laser aiming systems, night vision, flashlights, driveway probes, cameras, and video cameras. I try to get good rechargeable batteries for as many devices as possible. I have had good success with Sanyo Eneloops and Tenergy rechargeables. Of course you also need good chargers and some spares.

Lithium ion batteries are very much a part of our gadget world today from cell phones to laptops to power tools and electric vehicles. I have found the new external lithium-ion battery packs very handy to charge or run anything you can plug into them. In remote places or when traveling they have kept my cell phone and tablet going for the day without access

SMALL BATTERY TYPES: WHAT'S THE DIFFERENCE?

ALKALINE: These are the "standard" batteries that most people are familiar with, the onetime-use disposables; however, some can be recharged with varying results.

NICAD: Using nickel oxide hydroxide and cadmium, these are rechargeable, but newer technologies have made this battery nearly obsolete. However, some devices cannot use newer batteries. NiCads also suffer from what is called "memory"—that is the battery will lose capacity when the batteries are recharged after only being partially discharged.

NIMH: Using nickel metal hydride, this battery is similar to the NiCad battery. It offers higher energy density than NiCad, which gives it roughly twice the capacity of the NiCad. NiMH can also suffer from memory issues but not as severely as NiCad.

LITHIUM ION: These batteries produce the same power as NiMH but weigh 20–35 percent less. They do *not* suffer from the memory effect at all.

BATTERY COMPARISON (LEAD HOLDER)

to the grid. They can also be recharged with solar. I like charging DC-DC as it is more efficient then having inverters and transformers in the loop.

LARGER 12 VOLT BATTERIES

Many devices available for making life easier run off of 12 volts. People familiar with automotive, marine, and/or recreational vehicle (RV)

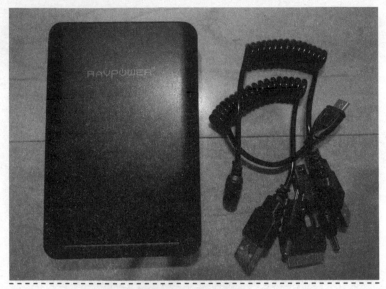

RAVPOWER 14000MAH

systems have a leg up on those who are only familiar with AC power that comes from the grid. In the 12 volt world there are lights, pumps, stoves, fans, coolers, freezers, and even microwaves that come in handy when the power goes out. Having a good 12 volt system is a great place to start when preparing. It is simple and there are plenty of pre-built systems on the market today.

12 VOLTS, 24 VOLTS, OR 48 VOLTS FOR YOUR BATTERIES?

Battery voltage is difficult to change after your system is built, so choose carefully at the start.

- 12 volt systems are the simplest and most standard, used in vehicles, RV, and boats. If you want a small simple power system, 12 volts will probably be easiest. You can power some devices with the battery's 12 volt DC current directly, and also get 120 volt AC (standard household power) with an inverter.

- 24 volt battery systems have some technical advantages. The higher the voltage, the longer the wire runs can be from your batteries to your pump or appliance. If you decide on 24 volts then use 24 volt solar panels and 24 volt charge controllers. You can use a 24 volt inverter to produce 120 volt AC power. Voltage converters are available to run 12 volt DC equipment from 24 volt batteries.

- 48 volts has great advantage if a longer wire run is unavoidable to reach a wind or hydro turbine. Larger, more powerful inverters are available in 48 volt. Typically a larger system capacity is the advantage of higher voltage, and 48 volt battery banks can have fewer strings. Fewer strings mean the batteries charge and discharge more evenly. Voltage converters are available to run 12 or 24 volt DC equipment from 48 volt batteries.

BATTERY BANKS

The reason for creating a battery bank is to store energy when it is being produced so that you can use it as needed. For example, when using solar energy you only have a short time to collect the energy, so you want to store every bit of it. When using a generator it is wise to run for only a few hours a day, conserving fuel, and then live off of the stored energy in the battery bank for the rest of the day. A battery bank is the result of joining two or more batteries together for a single application. What does this accomplish? Well, by connecting batteries, you can increase the voltage or amperage, or both. The ideal battery bank also is the simplest, consisting of a single series of cells that are sized for the job. This design minimizes maintenance and the possibility of random manufacturing defects.

BATTERY BANK CONFIGURATIONS

There are two main ways to connect your batteries together. One is putting your batteries in series; this will double the voltage and leave the amp-hour rating the same. The other is connecting them in parallel, which will double the amp-hour rating and leave the voltage the same. Depending on what voltage you need, what types of batteries you use, and what amp-hour rating you need you will have to use one or both of these connection methods.

CONNECTING BATTERIES IN SERIES

Below you will see examples of connecting two 6 volt 220 amp-hour batteries in series. Connecting batteries in this manner will double the voltage and sustain the same amp-hour rating.

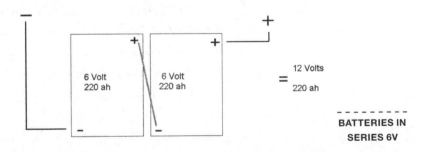

BATTERIES IN SERIES 6V

Here is the same type of connection with two 12 volt 100 amp-hour batteries

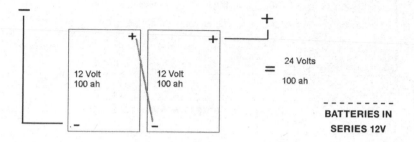

12 Volt
100 ah

12 Volt
100 ah

= 24 Volts
100 ah

BATTERIES IN
SERIES 12V

CONNECTING BATTERIES IN PARALLEL

Below you will see examples of connecting four 12 volt batteries in parallel. Connecting batteries in this manner will double the amp-hour rating and sustain the same voltage.

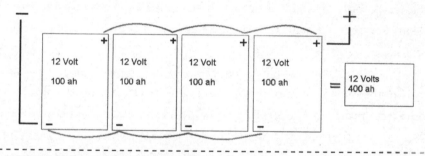

12 Volt
100 ah

12 Volt
100 ah

12 Volt
100 ah

12 Volt
100 ah

= 12 Volts
400 ah

12 VOLT BATTERIES CONNECTED IN PARALLEL TO FORM 12 VOLTS 400 AMP-HOURS

CONNECTING BATTERIES IN SERIES AND PARALLEL!

Below you will see examples of connecting batteries in series and parallel. The purpose of connecting your batteries in series and parallel is pertinent when you want to get a specific voltage when you only have a different voltage battery to begin with. It also allows you to increase the amp-hours and at the same time to equip your battery bank with more storage

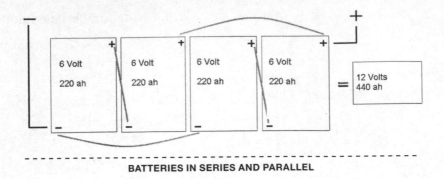

BATTERIES IN SERIES AND PARALLEL

capacity. Here we have four 6 volt batteries connected in series and parallel to form 12 volts 440 amp-hours.

Remember, electricity flows through a parallel connection just the same as it does in a single battery. It can't tell the difference. Therefore, you can connect two parallel connections in series as you would two batteries. Only one cable is needed, a bridge between a positive terminal from one parallel bank to a negative terminal from the other parallel bank.

There are many voltage configurations you can put your battery bank in, but the most common for solar and wind are 12, 24, and 48 volts. Most inverters and charge controllers come in these voltages. Hopefully these examples will give you some insight and knowledge into setting up your own battery bank.

BATTERY BANK CONNECTIONS

It's alright if a terminal has more than one cable connected to it. It is necessary to successfully construct these kinds of battery banks.

In theory, you can connect as many batteries together as you want. But when you start to construct a tangled mess of batteries and cables, it can be very confusing, and confusion can be dangerous. Keep in mind the requirements for your application, and stick to them. Also, use batteries of the same type and size. Avoid mixing and matching battery sizes wherever possible as the battery bank will not charge evenly if the batteries are mismatched.

Always remember to be safe, and keep track of your connections. If it helps, make a diagram of your battery banks before attempting to construct them. Use good quality battery interconnect cables. Many people use too light a gauge of wire. The smaller the wire, the greater the electrical resistance, and therefore the efficiency of your battery bank under load will be greatly diminished.

"FEW BATTERIES DIE A NATURAL DEATH, MOST ARE MURDERED"

I tell people that batteries like to be treated like your body when it comes to moisture and temperature. If you can keep them in a protected, cool, dry place, they will provide the best service. For example, temperature has a significant effect on lead-acid batteries. At 40 °F they will have 75 percent of rated capacity, and at 0 °F their capacity drops to 50 percent. The subject of batteries is mysterious to most and this section in no way addresses all the parameters that go into a robust battery system for your shelter. I want to stress that you need to take a systems approach to your shelter's power or you are going to make a lot of expensive mistakes.

Before investing in a power system that includes battery charging, consider the following:

1. Visit people who have off-grid battery systems in your area.

2. See what they are running for loads.

3. Take good notes.

4. Ask about maintenance requirements.

5. Buy a small portable solar system to gain an understanding of the components.

6. Oversize the system's capability by 20 percent.

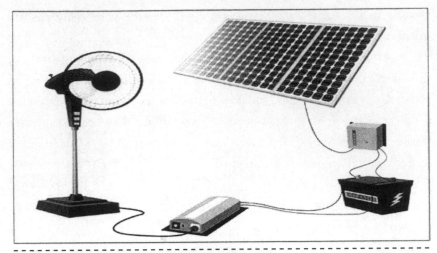

SOLAR POWER SETUP

Solar or Photovoltaic (PV) Systems

The sun is a great resource to take advantage of through the use of PV systems. You can start with something as small as a 5 watt solar panel to keep your cell phone topped off or you can install a 50 kW whole-house system that can synchronize with the grid, allowing you to zero out your power bill, have power in reserve, and even sell power back to your utility company. The cost of solar modules has dropped considerably in the last ten years making them more affordable. How does it all work?

1. Sun shining on solar modules produces DC current electricity. This power is stored in batteries while the sun is shining and can be quickly removed as needed.

2. An inverter converts the DC into AC for household use.

THE ANATOMY OF A PHOTOVOLTAIC SYSTEM:

SOLAR MODULES are used in groups to form what is called an array. These arrays can be mounted on roofs, poles, or ground mounts. The modules are connected together with wires that junction in a combiner box. At the

SOLAR ARRAY

combiner, larger wires are attached to take the power to the utility room or building where the batteries are stored.

A **CHARGE CONTROLLER** is used to receive the power from the array, wind, or hydro generator. It is typically a wall-mounted unit that controls the flow of power to the batteries. To prevent battery damage from overcharging, the charge control automatically cuts back, stops, or diverts the power when batteries become full. A charge control may have manual control switches and may have meters or lights to show the status of the charging process.

CHARGE CONTROLLER

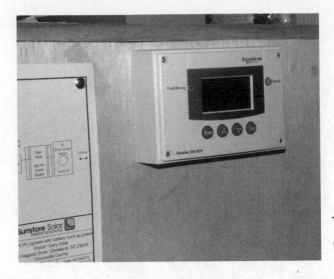

SOLAR
CHARGE
METER

METERS, such as the gas and temperature gauges in a car, are necessary to show that everything is working correctly. Solar charge indicating meters are often built into the charge controller to confirm the charging process instantly. Other meters show how much power is being consumed, and confirm how much power is available. These battery system monitors can be located in the power room, or at a convenient spot in the home for easier monitoring.

BATTERIES receive, store, and release DC electrical energy, and can instantly supply large surges of stored electricity as needed to start or run heavy power appliances that the solar panels or hydroelectric generator alone could not power. This large power capability can be a fire hazard, so fuses and circuit breakers on every circuit connected to a battery are essential. Battery size is chosen for both surge power requirements and for the amount of reserve power needed to get through times of low production. This time period is often referred to as *days of autonomy.*

INVERTERS are the components with the most electronics and therefore can be the weakest link in a system if they are not protected from power surges, lightning strikes, and potential EMP (electromagnetic pulse) events. Inverters convert DC power stored in batteries to 120 volt

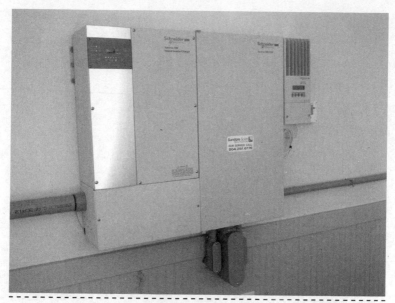

INVERTER CHARGER

AC, standard household power. Short, heavy cables with a large fuse or circuit breaker carry battery power to the inverter. After conversion to AC, power from the inverter usually connects into the circuit breaker box of the house in place of utility lines. The house breaker box routes power to lights, appliances, and outlets of the house as needed.

On larger whole-house systems, **INVERTER CHARGERS** incorporate a DC to AC inverter, a battery charger, and an AC auto-transfer switch. They are the foundation for battery-based residential and commercial applications. Many of them are capable of being grid interactive or grid independent and can operate with generators and renewable energy sources to provide full-time or back-up power.

AN ENGINE GENERATOR producing 120 volt or 120/240 volt AC power can also be a part of the system. This is a second source of AC power and a backup for charging the battery bank when there is a lack of solar or wind power. Just starting the generator begins the standby inverter charging process. The best generators start automatically or by push button from the house.

ARMSTRONG POWER SYSTEMS GENERATOR

A generator is located outside, usually in its own building for health and safety reasons. AC power from the generator goes through a circuit breaker, then is wired into the power room to run battery chargers as well as supply the AC power to the house whenever the generator runs. We have found that it is easier to install a generator and automatic transfer switch to a home separate from the solar or alternative energy system. This allows for larger generators to pull all the loads in a home when the power goes out. When the generator switches on, the inverter charger senses its AC power and uses it to top off the batteries. So, in essence the solar system sees the generator as grid power and uses it accordingly.

FUSES OR CIRCUIT BREAKERS are necessary in all DC wiring between the batteries and other power system components described. They prevent fire and equipment damage in the event of a malfunction. Breakers may be separate components in their own box, or they might be built into a

**MANUAL GRID
DISCONNECT**

power center. In contrast, the AC breaker box for household wiring is part of the house wiring. Today, many customers ask for extra surge protection due to the threat of EMP or even cyber attacks to the grid. Anything that can cause an electrical surge in the grid can wipe out any or all electronic equipment in its path. Protecting your equipment can be quite costly but there are companies such as Polyphaser and Transector that specialize in protecting and/or hardening your equipment from these surges. Most of the time the hardening solution is more expensive than the original system components. As an alternative solution, but one that doesn't guarantee protection, I recommend installing a manual disconnect from the grid that can be thrown if you get word of an imminent event. I also recommend installing as many lightning arrestors and surge protectors as you can to protect your investment.

Now, let's look at the different types of photovoltaic systems.

PORTABLE SYSTEMS

These systems, such as the SUNRNR system that we sell on our website, are ideal for someone who wants to have back-up power but can't have the system visible for either security reasons or because, where they live, the Homeowners Association's restrictions do not allow for solar power. These also make great systems to take with you if you have an RV or an RV is part of your bug-out strategy. Some preppers even have multiple portable systems instead of one large system so that they have backups if one fails. I have used small portable systems since my first experience with one during Hurricane Katrina relief efforts in 2005. I took two panels coupled

THE SUNRNR
110/120, A
PORTABLE SOLAR
GENERATOR

to two charge controllers, two deep cycle batteries, and two inverters with our gear. Every day the small DIY systems kept things such as our radios and phones running and even allowed us to have coffee in the morning!

The preparedness market is flooded with portable systems, so I encourage you to do your homework. Many manufacturers make grandiose claims about what their systems can produce, but that is usually based on how much energy can be quickly removed from the battery. This is not acceptable to me as the only true sustainable energy you have is coming from the solar panel. What I mean by this is that you may be able to extract a lot of energy at once through the inverter, but then it might take you days to replace that energy via the solar panel. Do your homework when it comes to these systems.

Once you purchase a portable solar system, do not leave it in the box on a shelf for the "rainy day"! Open it, set it up, and begin to use it on a

KILL A WATT

daily basis so that you will not be surprised that it will not run your freezer for more than a day.

GRID-TIE ONLY SYSTEM

This is the most common application today, and is basically the simplest in terms of components and expense. Components consist of modules, an inverter, racking, conduit, wire, and disconnects. This system operates parallel to the utility grid and only operates when the utility voltage is present. If your local utility offers *net metering*, then the energy your system produces can be sold back to them. This used to be called running your meter backward. The new smart meters determine how much power is being used or produced and in which direction the flow of electricity is going. For disaster preparedness we do not recommend grid tie. We have had several customers who had grid-tie systems installed only later to realize that their investment would be rendered useless if the grid went down. It's possible to convert these systems to Grid-Tie Battery Backups but that requires jumping through many hoops and adds complexity and inefficiencies to the overall system.

GRID-TIE-BATTERY BACKUP

Just as the name implies, this allows us to add storage capacity to a grid-tie system with a battery bank, to operate electrical devices when the utility voltage is not present. Careful consideration of critical loads is essential to battery bank design. This is the system we suggest for folks who want to have power when the grid power is interrupted. I prefer this type of system because while the grid is working the grid itself is used to keep the battery banks fully charged when solar power or any other alternative energy system's power is not producing. Then, when the grid goes down, your alternative energy source charges the bank. With this system you can also net meter the power back to the grid once the batteries are fully charged and you are producing extra power. The goal for many of our customers is a power bill that is greatly reduced or is at zero each month.

STAND-ALONE SYSTEMS

These run with no connection to the utility grid. Careful consideration of daily power consumption and battery bank condition is a must. Many

SOLAR PANEL INSTALLATION CONSIDERATIONS:

- Set your panel angles at the latitude of your GPS location. You can add 15 degrees for winter and subtract 15 degrees for summer.

- Pole mounts offer the greatest flexibility in capturing the most sun year-round because the array can be adjusted on two axes so that you can make seasonal adjustments to capture the most sun possible.

- Roof mounts are typically the least expensive way to mount your modules but the least flexible for adjusting to the sun's seasonal path changes.

- Take the time to understand the path that the sun takes, especially at the summer and winter solstices. The winter solstice will typically be the worst day for solar with the highest amount of shading.

times these are also called hybrid systems since they have other back-up sources, such as wind or a generator. If your electric use is high, it can be quite expensive to get 100 percent of your electricity from solar or other renewable resources.

Wind Power

Wind can be used in at least three ways to help ease dependence on the utility grid. There are wind turbines for making electricity, windpumps for lifting water out of a well, and windmills for producing mechanical power to do things like grind grains. Within this section, we'll discuss wind turbines as they can be a nice complement to a solar battery back-up system. This is because in the summer, wind speeds are typically lower but sun production is ample; in the winter, when the sun is lower in the sky, wind speeds are higher so overall power production can average out nicely.

WIND SPEED VS. POWER: WHAT'S THE DIFFERENCE?

Wind speed is the rate at which air flows past a point above the earth's surface. Wind speed can be quite variable.

Wind power is a measure of the energy available in the wind. It is a function of the cube (third power) of the wind speed. If the wind speed is doubled, power in the wind increases by a factor of eight.

Before considering a wind turbine for your location, consult the charts for your area from the NREL (National Renewable Energy Laboratory). There are also wind simulation tools that can be used to place turbines on your exact site so you can see if a wind turbine makes sense. A wind site widget from Bergey.com can be used as a site evaluator. Just put in your address and drag the turbine to the potential install site and it will let you know if wind is for you.

If you live in a high wind area then a wind turbine can provide you far more energy at a lower investment than a solar array.

If you have good wind speed at times but not at others consider a smaller micro wind turbine instead of the big expensive install.

My two cents on wind after being involved with a 7.5 kW system is this. Do your research on the latest greatest technologies. There are so many types of turbines, and one of the biggest issues for me was the random noise of the blades. At times of high wind I wanted to duck as the blades sounded like a boomerang coming toward my head.

Once you have chosen your turbine, it's important to note that the higher you can place the turbine, the less turbulence you'll get. The lower the turbulence the more power the turbine can capture.

Erecting a tower is the hardest part of wind systems. There are several types of towers ranging from the guyed lattice to the monopole. Again, do your research to determine the best tower for your location and turbine.

Experienced crane operators and riggers are needed for the taller tower installs.

Hydro Power

Like wind power, hydro is a great complement to solar because your higher hydro production times are during the fall, winter, and spring months when solar production is lower. Among the essential sources of renewable energy, hydro has the lowest production costs. An advantage of small-scale water plants (or micro hydro systems) is their low impact and disturbance factors for the environment. I am contacted often to make assessments of streams and other waterways to see if they will supply adequate energy to run some type of turbine or wheel for making electricity. The two primary factors of hydroelectric power are head (the water's vertical drop) and flow rate. A good site needs a combination of these two. Higher head sites are typically more cost-effective installations since you can use smaller pipe and less water as gravity is on your side. Ideally, you want a stream that is a series of tumbling waterfalls. A waterway that is relatively flat won't do much for you—if there is no change in elevation then there is no power.

A good home-scale system might have a vertical drop in the range of forty to two hundred feet. Water is delivered to the turbine through what is called a Penstock. This can be a sluice (or gate), or a pipe that controls water flow to the turbine. This water flows through nozzles that

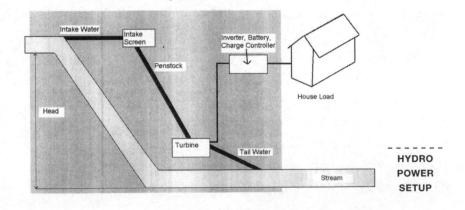

PELTON WHEEL (ZEDH)

concentrate the water onto spoon-shaped blades that are attached to a wheel. The wheel spins an alternator that produces electricity.

Micro hydro systems are most simply categorized by three types of system designs (though there are many variations within these groups):

- High head low flow site: recommended with a Pelton type generator

- Medium head higher flow site: recommended with a Turgo runner type generator

- Low head high volume: recommended with a propeller or wheel type generator

I have been fortunate to have two micro hydro sites near me where I have spent hours studying, asking questions, and learning all the ins and outs of what works and what doesn't. One system produces 45 kW/hr at a flow rate of eight hundred gallons per minute and a five hundred-foot head into an OSSBERGER turbine. This runs a Christian retreat center

with a lodge and multiple homes and maintenance center. The other
system uses a 4-nozzle Harris turbine and provides power for a bug-out
cabin in the mountains. It uses a Pelton wheel to capture all the energy
from water falling seventy-four feet and up to three hundred gallons per
minute. There are many hydro systems on YouTube and if you are looking
for design help for your micro hydro project you can contact us or Langs-
ton's Alternative Power in South Carolina.

One important issue that comes up when evaluating a site is that
many times the source of water for a micro hydro site is also the property

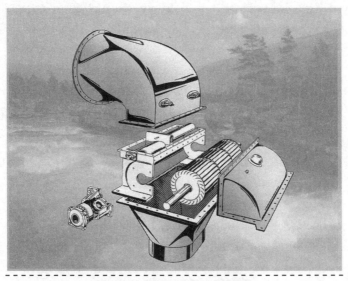

THE OSSBERGER TURBINE (PC21)

line between two neighbors. Make sure there is enough water for your project because if you "rob" all the water through your Penstock your neighbor will not appreciate the fact that you have changed their beautiful stream. Even though the site might be perfect for production, it might not be allowed by the neighbor.

Gasification

A friend of mine told me that vehicles in Europe were running on wood during World War II, and I was immediately off and researching. I learned that pyrolized wood produces a vapor or gas that can run in almost any internal combustion engine. Pyrolysis is the process of breaking down a substance with heat. This is an oxygen-starved process so there is no burning. As I looked into this new world of renewable energy production, I was hooked. I bought a small gasification cookstove to see if all the claims were true. As I said before, my middle name growing up was "get wood," so as I watched this small simple device burn wood so efficiently I was intrigued to say the least. The small stove and my research led me to all sorts of contraptions (called gasifiers) that can be used to convert biomass into producer or syngas, which is a usable fuel for running engines.

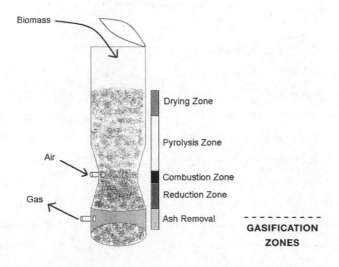

MY GASIFIER

MY EXPERIENCE WITH GASIFICATION

I set out to see if I could produce enough electricity to run my home off of a gasified generator. The prototype Victory Gasworks gasifier arrived at my shop on my birthday, and I was like a little kid on Christmas day putting it together. When I fired it up and a two-foot blue flame shot out of the flare, I was excited to say the least. During that time I searched for a generator to match the gasifier. The displacement of the engine and the displacement of the gasifier must be matched. The size of the gasifier, specifically the hearth, has been arrived at empirically over the years. The syngas is approximately 20 percent hydrogen and 20 percent carbon monoxide. That combination can run any gasoline type engine. My 1970 25 kW generator would be perfect. The day I filled the gasifier with white oak blocks and ran that engine for two hours straight I was dancing around like I had just discovered fire!

Since that day I have run my home, driven my truck, and operated a wood splitter on wood alone. I dared my brother to bring me his Harley-Davidson motorcycle and said I could get it running off of wood in less than two hours and we did! Now, I make it sound fun and glamorous but I will tell you that without a high-density wood at moisture content under 20 percent all this "fun" wouldn't have happened. I spent weeks and weeks tweaking homemade carburetors and making charcoal filters and drying wood to get the gasifier to perform correctly. I call gasification the "mad max" of preparations because it is my go to if there is no fossil fuel to be found in a crisis situation. I have all these projects documented on YouTube under the Engineer775 Practical Preppers channel — check it out for more information.

> **TYPES OF BIOMASS**
>
> Wood ■ Crops ■ Garbage
> Alcohol fuels ■ Landfill gas

GASIFICATION: THE WAY OF THE FUTURE?

Gasification is not just for World War II anymore. Due to tough EPA restrictions on wood-burning devices, woodstove and outdoor boiler manufacturers have had to turn to gasification (as we mentioned p. 128). Many states are outlawing old-style woodstoves. Another amazing thing going on in the renewable energy world is the production of liquid fuels from biomass. Syngas can be converted to liquid fuels like diesel and there are several plants in the United States and around the world that do so. It was first done in 1925 via the Fischer–Tropsch reaction. The process is a collection of chemical reactions that converts a mixture of carbon monoxide and hydrogen into liquid hydrocarbons. I have that project sketched out and look forward to the day where I can put biomass in the gasifier and remove liquid diesel for my car on the other end.

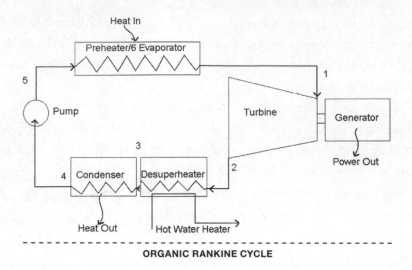

ORGANIC RANKINE CYCLE

Heat Engines

There are many other ways to make power such as steam engines, Stirling engines, wave generators, bio digesters, fuel cells, and the list goes on. I want to close out this power resupply section with one that I think has tremendous potential, and that is the heat engine. A heat engine is a system that converts heat energy to mechanical work. I believe the heat engine will be the next thing to revolutionize power production and the transportation industry. There are already engines out there like the Cyclone that can use any fuel type and produce real usable power. There is more energy to be produced from the waste heat by-product of power-generation plants and industrial manufacturing processes than all alternative sources such as solar, wind, and hydro combined.

At the time of writing this book I have constructed a prototype ORC. Not the type of ORC you find in *The Lord of the Rings* but an Organic Rankine Cycle. The working principle of the organic Rankine cycle is the same as that of the steam engine. An ORC is a heat engine that converts heat into mechanical work. In an ORC a low boiling point refrigerant fluid is pumped to a boiler where it is evaporated, and then passed through a turbine where it is finally recondensed and the cycle repeats. The goal is to produce enough power to run an American home with a process that has emissions that pass all EPA standards and its fuel source is renewable biomass. Two side benefits are that it is quiet and hot water is the by-product.

Conservation

Whatever process you choose to resupply energy during a time of crisis, your best money spent is on conservation practices ahead of time. Performing an energy audit of your shelter can reveal many ways in which your energy usage can be diminished. Changing my incandescent lightbulbs to compact fluorescents and LEDs saved me $50 per month. Replacing my twenty-year-old chest freezer saved me a 250 watt solar panel's worth of daily energy production. If you take the time to reduce your energy use at the outset, you will lower the load requirements on your resupply plan down the road.

Tax Credits and Rebates

One big consideration before investing in a renewable energy resupply plan is to see what is available for tax credits, rebates, and even grants in your area. Some resources to consider are www.dsireusa.org/solar/ and for homesteads and small farms look into www.nrcs.usda.gov.

MEDICAL
How Do I Fix It?

A REMINDER

The information in this book is not intended to be a substitute for professional medical advice, diagnosis, or treatment. Never disregard professional medical advice or delay seeking medical treatment because of something you have read in this book.

Disasters come in all shapes and sizes—from superstorms to cancer. My wife, Lori, has worked as a pharmacist in both hospital and retail for more than twenty years. Through the years Lori has shared many tales of human suffering with me. Unfortunately, a good deal of these tragedies are self-inflicted and stem from lack of personal preparedness. If I were attempting to keep a car in good working order for eighty years, I would need to put a decent amount of time and money in maintaining the engine, body, and tires. Very few people invest in keeping their bodies "tuned up," with the expectation they will live for many years. Due to this lack of routine maintenance, not many people actually achieve either the health or longevity they desire. Of course, in cases of major natural disasters, surviving the dangers associated with the event becomes paramount. This chapter has a two-fold goal: to walk readers through storing items integral for survival during emergency scenarios and to help readers prepare medically by seeking personal fitness and good nutrition.

MEDICAL STORAGE

Basic Medical Supplies

Every household should have a first aid kit. First aid kits must be small and portable for the majority of short-term uses. A small kit should be able to address minor wounds, bites, and discomforts. This is different from a medic bag, which would address more significant life-saving issues. Personal responsibility separates these, too. If you have minimal medical training, you need to stick with items you can safely use. There are some medical items that can be harmful if used inappropriately, so medic bags should be reserved for EMTs, paramedics, RNs, or other medically licensed personnel familiar with more advanced techniques. While we currently have decent Good Samaritan laws in place in the United States, there are also no guarantees you won't be sued (or worse), even if you had the best intentions. This is important to remember in WROL (Without Rule Of Law) situations, too, as sooner or later civility will be restored and the justice system back up and running. First, do no harm.

A SMALL KIT SHOULD CONTAIN THESE ITEMS:

- Gloves—to protect you from the patient's bodily fluids
- Bandages—assorted sizes—two or three of each
- Sterile gauze 2 x 2, 4 x 4, triangle bandage

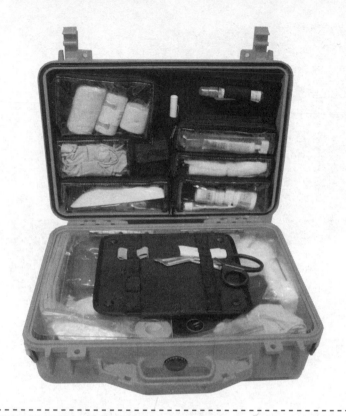

WELL-EQUIPPED FIRST AID KIT (RILEY HUNTLEY, HUNTLEY PHOTOGRAPHY)

- Adhesive tape
- Butterfly closures or Steri-Strips
- Blunt end scissors for removing clothes or cutting gauze
- Triple antibiotic ointment
- Antiseptic wipes—benzalkonium chloride
- Alcohol wipes
- Two tabs each of acetaminophen, ibuprofen, aspirin, diphenhydramine, loperamide
- Insect bite (ammonia) treatment

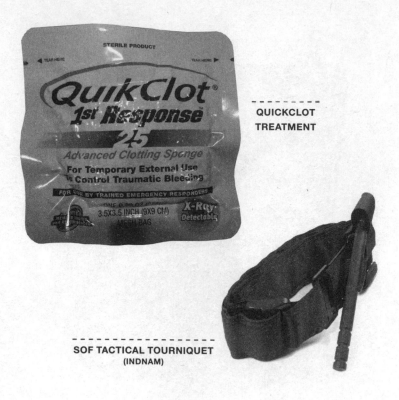

QUICKCLOT
TREATMENT

SOF TACTICAL TOURNIQUET
(INDNAM)

- Emergency space blanket

- QuickClot

- C-A-T tourniquet or SOF tactical tourniquet (preferred)

This last item may seem advanced for a basic kit but should always be included in the bag of easily portable materials. I speak with many knowledgeable people concerning life-saving treatments and we all agree, tourniquets offer the biggest bang for the buck. The best way to prevent the mortality associated with massive bleeding is to stop bleeding as soon as possible. There has even been an abdominal tourniquet recently approved for use in the United States for abdominal gunshots or other bleeding trauma. Tourniquets are extremely easy to use. They are applied 2–4 inches above the wound on the affected limb to stop bleeding. The wide

EMERGENCY BLANKET (MARKUS BRUNNER)

web band compresses the blood vessels. The tourniquet is tightened as much as possible by tightening the windlass until blood flow stops. Checking for absence of pulse below the tourniquet will verify blood supply is reduced. This reduces blood loss, which in turn reduces or eliminates hypovolemic shock, one of the major threats posed by traumatic injury. SOF tourniquets can be applied one handed and have never failed in Army Institute of Surgical Research testing. These are available online from Tactical Medical Solutions. Consider the five to ten minutes it takes to learn how to use a tourniquet as time well spent. Never apply a tourniquet to the neck—yeah, we all know someone who would do that. There are plenty of YouTube videos on applying tourniquets—try Zombiestrategic or SkinnyMedic channels. Also, the Red Cross routinely offers classes on basic first aid, as do local hospitals and community colleges.

QuickClot does what is says. It is available over the counter in various package sizes. The powder instantly stops bleeding.

The emergency space blanket is placed over any injured person who is shivering. After a traumatic injury, shock can set in, which will cause shivering even in a warm environment. Loss of body temperature is a serious threat to a traumatized person and can reduce overall survival rate. If an injured person is lying on the cold pavement or is wet, body heat loss will occur rapidly and the victim will begin shunting blood from their extremities and become acidotic—a condition far more difficult to treat than to prevent. Acidosis is a condition that can develop from trauma and blood loss and is an important predictor of death secondary to clotting issues. [source: www.medscape.com/viewarticle/725859_5 Role of Fibrinogen in Trauma-induced Coagulopathy. D. Fries, W. Z. Martini *British Journal of Anaesthesia*. 2010; 105(2): 116–21.]

Acetaminophen is a mild painkiller and an antipyretic fever reducer. A typical adult dose is 650–1000 mg (depending on whether you have 325-mg tabs or 500-mg tabs). These are available without a prescription and can be found in individually wrapped packs for ease of use and storage.

Ibuprofen is a mild painkiller and also an antipyretic. A typical adult dose is 400–800 mg. It is available as a 200 mg tablet. These are available without a prescription and can also be found individually wrapped. An important note about ibuprofen: Do not give this to a person who claims an allergy to NSAIDs or aspirin, as cross-reactivity has been observed. Verify allergies before dosing.

Aspirin is a mild painkiller and mild blood thinner. Historically it was a fever reducer, although it is not used this way anymore as there are risks associated with giving it to children with fever, including Reye's Syndrome. Aspirin should be given to anyone whom you suspect is having a clotting event. Symptoms of such an incident include: crushing chest pain (heart attack) or stroke symptoms (confusion, inability to speak, drooping face, and the inability to move one side of the body). One 325 mg tablet is sufficient to thin the blood while you are getting help. Do not give aspirin to anyone with a history of allergy to NSAIDs or aspirin.

Diphenhydramine (Benadryl) is an antihistamine used for treating allergic reactions. A typical adult dosage is 25–50 mg, roughly one to two capsules. It can reduce swelling as well as reduce dizziness, and cause drowsiness. Diphenhydramine can help with insect bites as well as hives or other allergic skin reactions. Do not give to anyone with a history of allergy to it.

Loperamide (Imodium) is an antidiarrheal. A typical adult dose is 2 mg (one capsule) initially, then one capsule after every loose bowel movement up to eight capsules per day. It is rare to use more than a few doses of this as it is a very powerful medication.

Alcohol and antiseptic wipes are for preliminary wound cleaning. Alcohol stings more when introduced to open wounds. Have some of both.

Triple antibiotic ointment is useful for scratches and abrasions. It is greasy and useful when avoiding scab formation, especially for mild burns or facial cuts. Scabs contribute to forming scar tissue. Some people's tissue will develop a red rim where the ointment has been applied. The neomycin component of the ointment often causes this. Switching to just polymixin and bacitracin (Polysporin is a brand in the United States) will often solve this reaction.

Blunt end scissors are useful for removing clothing. Do not use regular scissors as another trauma may be introduced.

Butterfly closures are great for holding external wounds together and are much safer than suturing without experience or licensure. Please remember that if you decide to close a wound, in most cases you are also closing in thousands of bacteria that will begin replicating immediately. I strongly recommend either storing antibiotics or becoming knowledgeable in herbal remedies or essential oils used to treat infection. Two of my favorite resources in print are:

- *The Survival Medicine Handbook: A Guide for When Medical Help Is Not on the Way* by Joseph Alton, MD, and Amy Alton, ARNP. Doom and Bloom (revised and enlarged) 2013.

- *Herbal Antibiotics: Natural Alternatives for Treating Drug-Resistant Bacteria* by Stephen Harrod Buhner. Storey Publishing, LLC (2nd edition) 2012.

Sterile gauze and bandages clean and protect the wound. Adhesive tape can hold larger bandages.

Advanced Medical Supplies

A medic's bag is more extensive and may include the following:

- Stethoscope
- Blood pressure cuff
- Antibiotics
- IV fluids
- Bandages of many varieties
- Splints
- Oscillococcinum
- Abdominal aortic tourniquets
- Chest seal such as Halo seals

This increased level of preparedness should be matched by increased education in medicine. There are local classes in most hospitals for basic EMT training. Those with licenses already, such as registered nurses or

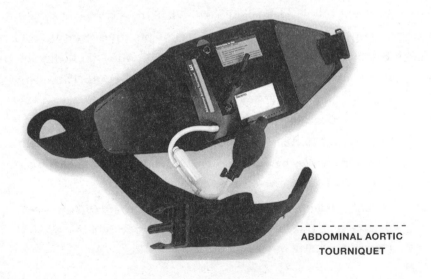

**ABDOMINAL AORTIC
TOURNIQUET**

paramedics, may have far more extensive bags prepared. I am reluctant to dictate all that goes into the medic's bag as his or her own expertise will dictate what direction the preparations will go. A stethoscope and cuff will be more useful for those with an internal medicine education, while IV fluids and bandages are more for trauma applications. One thing almost everyone will agree on is the use and availability of antibiotics.

Infection

Antibiotics and vaccines are the twentieth-century medical miracles. Now in the twenty-first century, bacterial resistance will end antibiotic usage very soon. Because of resistance, not all antibiotics work for all infections. It is a well-known fact in the prepper community that fish antibiotics, available without a prescription, are identical in composition to their human counterparts. There are apps such as iPharmacy available for smart phones that identify

CEFAZOLIN

prescription medicines, and show that the appearance and identification markings on the fish antibiotics are identified by the apps as being the same as the ones for human use.

Before using antibiotics, it is important to try to determine if the infection is viral or bacterial. In general, viral infections produce low-grade fevers (under 100 °F) and increased mucus production. Also, throat tissue doesn't become "beefy red" as with many bacterial infections. Of course there are tropical diseases and other rare infections that break this rule, but for average conditions—no pandemics—it holds true. While we at Practical Preppers do not encourage practicing medicine without a license, we must recognize the possibility that disasters can cut individuals off from medical care. First, do no harm. Whenever possible, it is always best to seek professional medical care first.

Where an infection is located usually determines the type of antibiotic used. In the crudest sense, infections can be separated by above and below the belly button. Infections above tend to be *gram-positive,* a term used by microbiologists to describe the permeability of the bacterial wall. Infections below the belly button tend to be *gram-negative*. Since each antibiotic has a specific way it invades the bacteria, the cell wall permeability determines which antibiotic works against each bacteria type.

Respiratory infections include any infection along the respiratory tract. This would be, from the head down: sinus, ear, throat, bronchi, and lungs. Airways are a superhighway into the human body and usually have mucus coverings to capture invaders. At the start of an invasion, the body produces extra mucus, seen as runny nose and coughing. Later, fever (usually over 102 °F) and pain can occur. A bacterial sore throat, such as strep throat, is characterized by a beefy red throat with white pus spots, a furry tongue, pain upon swallowing, and a temperature usually over 102 °F.

Remember antipyretics such as acetaminophen or ibuprofen will reduce core temperature by 1 to 1.5 degrees Fahrenheit, so consider this if your patient has been medicated with either in the previous six hours. Azithromycin, a relative of erythromycin, is a fine choice for an upper respiratory infection. It is safe for children when the dosage is adjusted. Adult dosage is 500 mg day one, followed by 250 mg every day for four more days. It should not be given to anyone claiming allergy to it or clarithromycin, or erythromycin.

Amoxicillin with or without clavulanate is also excellent. An adult dosage of amoxicillin is 500 mg three times daily for ten days, or 875 mg twice daily for ten days. Fewer bacterial strains are resistant to amoxicillin with clavulanate and it is dosed similiarly. Always determine if the patient is allergic to any antibiotics, and do not challenge them with any in that class or family if they report they are. Pneumonia is extremely serious with a high mortality rate if untreated. Ciprofloxacin or Levofloxacin are great choices, again as long as the patient is not allergic. Adult dosage is 750 mg twice a day for ciprofloxacin and 750 mg once daily for Levofloxacin. These drugs are not labeled for use for patients under fourteen years old.

For infections below the belly button, such as urinary tract infection, sulfamethoxazole/trimethoprim is excellent. Roughly 10 percent of the population is allergic to this drug, so screen for allergy and also for first-degree relatives with a history of allergy to it. This drug can cause nasty allergic reactions including severe skin rash, and you certainly do not want to deal with a life-threatening allergy if you do not have access to medical care. Adult dose is 800 mg/160 mg twice daily for seven days. Symptoms of a UTI include urinary urgency and frequency with minimal output, pelvic pain, low-grade temperature, cloudy urine. If the infection is not treated it can progress (about 50 percent of the time) to a kidney infection. Those symptoms include as above plus flank pain, bloody urine, and a temperature over 102 °F. Ciprofloxacin can also be used for a UTI at 250–500 mg twice daily for ten days.

Infectious diarrhea is a worldwide problem that claims many lives each year. It is caused by ingesting contaminated water or food. Pandemic infections such as cholera and salmonella can ravage a human so quickly that antibiotics do not have time to work. This is where complications from dehydration caused by excessive vomiting and/or diarrhea are actually what will kill the patient. In the United States, the natural inclination is to start IV fluids. If you are truly cut off from medical care, you most likely will not have IV fluids. Also, unless you are trained and licensed, you will run the risk of harm and/or litigation once the catastrophe is over. The World Health Organization has developed an oral rehydration solution recipe that literally saves thousands of lives yearly. It is cheap and can be made with items basic to most households.

World Health Organization Rehydration Solution

$3/8$ tsp salt (sodium chloride)

$1/4$ tsp Morton Salt Substitute (potassium chloride)

$1/2$ tsp baking soda (sodium bicarbonate)

2 tbsp + 2 tsp sugar (sucrose)

Add tap water to make 1 liter

OPTIONAL: NutraSweet- or Splenda-based flavoring of choice, to taste

Directions

1. Add the dry ingredients to a 1-liter bottle.

2. Add enough water to make a final volume of 1 liter; mix well.

3. If desired, add NutraSweet- or Splenda-based flavoring, to taste. Mix well.

4. Sip as directed by your physician.

5. Discard after twenty-four hours.

Contains 27 grams of sucrose, 70 mEq (milliequivalent) per liter of sodium, 20 mEq per liter of potassium and 30 mEq per liter of bicarbonate. The final osmolarity is approximately 245 mOsm (millismole) per liter.

This solution should be given to the patient as 1 teaspoonful every 5 minutes for 1 hour or until no diarrhea or vomiting occurs. Then increase to 2 teaspoons every 5 minutes for 1 hour until no diarrhea or vomiting occurs. Then 3 teaspoons every 5 minutes for 1 hour. The patient at this point should be able to sip on demand. If they get worse, start over with 1 teaspoonful every 5 minutes for 1 hour.

I personally saw how well this recipe worked when my daughters became very sick with an intestinal infection that was being passed around at school. Their friends were sick for about five days and were going to the hospital for IV fluids. While all three daughters became sick and stayed sick for the five days, they remained well enough hydrated by using this recipe. I can tell you they weren't fond of the taste, but they were glad to avoid the hospital visit.

Skin infections need to be treated a little differently from the other infections. Cephalexin, unless the person is allergic to it, is a good choice for infected insect stings and other cellulitis or cuts or scrapes. Cephalexin is dosed 500 mg three or four times daily for ten days for skin infection. MRSA, methicillin-resistant *Staphylococcus aureus*, is now a common skin ailment in community-acquired infections. These potentially serious skin infections are resistant to most antibiotics.

Sulfamethoxazole/trimethoprim 800 mg/160 mg twice daily is what

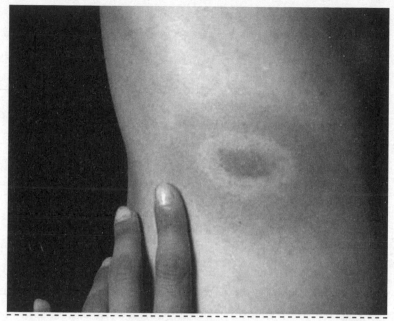

TICK BITE (HANNAH GARRISON)

most practitioners are now using while skin cultures are pending. MRSA can come in the form of boils or weeping, crusting wounds. The skin infection spreads rapidly. Doxycycline can also be considered at an adult dose of 100 mg twice daily for ten days. Doxycycline gets good skin penetration and works well on tick bites to protect against Lyme disease and Rocky Mountain Spotted Fever (RMSF) rickettsia.

Vaccines

Vaccines can be controversial, especially with parents of young children. If they are offensive to you, please skip this section. I have no desire to offend. Because personal preparedness can save so much suffering, I do recommend everyone have tetanus vaccinations at five-year intervals unless they are allergic to it. Tetanus or lockjaw is a horrible disease characterized by prolonged muscle contraction. It requires tremendous medical resources to treat it and still carries significant mortality. It is rarely seen in developed countries due to the high rate of vaccination. Let's keep it that way! Also, currently there are several childhood diseases on the upswing. Pertussis (whooping cough) can be effectively treated with a cheap and easy vaccination. Pertussis presents as a bad cold in an adult, but can devastate a young child. Pertussis causes severe respiratory distress in children and can be deadly, especially in the under two months set, as they cannot be vaccinated. The CDC website has the most up-to-date recommendations for vaccination.

I am occasionally asked if I would get vaccinated for yellow fever, as prior to the twentieth century, yellow fever was a significant cause of death in the Southern United States. I can tell you I have far more serious concerns about malaria and dengue fever in the South than yellow fever. Unfortunately, there are no vaccines for either at the time of this writing. Antimalarials are available but expensive. Quinine offers little protection as most strains of malaria have become resistant. Dengue fever requires supportive care. It is a hemorrhagic fever and has spread from Africa to Mexico and South America in the past ten years. My recommendations for these diseases spread by mosquitoes are prevention by storing repellent containing DEET and mosquito netting.

Injuries

Suturing should be reserved for trained personnel. There are a multitude of suture types, and some of them, such as braided, can shelter bacteria and offer crevices for replication and do more harm than good. Sutures require putting more holes into the patient, introducing more bacteria below the skin, and increasing risk of infection in environments that lack sterility. It also raises the question of whether some sort of anesthetic should be used, as most children and adults won't take well to being stabbed with a needle multiple times near a wound. "Practicing medicine without a license" in a WROL situation can still be prosecuted once the legal system is working.

Steri-Strips or butterfly closures with Dermabond or superglue are an alternative to suturing. Close the wound in such a way that drainage can occur at the edges. Crush wounds should *not* be sutured, as they swell significantly. Keep them clean and dry. Once a wound is closed, antibiotics should be considered. See skin-infection recommendations above. The wound should be watched for signs of infection. Green or yellow discharge, foul smell, swelling, and redness in and around the wound are all signs of infection. The wound should be cleaned and allowed to drain. Keep strips or closures on the wound for five to seven days for relatively shallow wounds, and up to ten days on deeper wounds. The tissue should show a pink edge and some scar tissue, which looks and feels "ropey."

Childbirth

Childbirth without access to modern medicine may become one of the least enjoyable experiences in a collapse situation. I tell my clients to look to the past to gauge what life would be like without a power grid. During the American Revolution, the maternal mortality rate, the measurement of death in pregnant women, was 2–4 percent per pregnancy. Since the average family had six children, the cumulative rate could approach 25 percent, or one in four women. If there is even one woman of childbearing age in your neighborhood, it will behoove you to invest in at least one childbirth book. I don't mean the entertaining ones that show every week of development of the baby, but rather the detailed ones on labor and

UMBILICAL CORD CLAMP
(ROGER MCLASSUS)

delivery. Having a midwife or an RN with labor and delivery experience as a neighbor is priceless. Here is a list of childbirth supplies to stock:

- Underpads
- Plastic sheets
- Sanitary pads
- Perineal irrigation bottle
- Gauze 4 x 4
- Bulb syringe
- Gloves (several pairs)
- Iodine solution 10 percent
- Two cord clamps
- Baby hat
- Receiving blanket
- Soap/hand sanitizer
- Scapel or umbilical scissors, sterile

The website www.1cascade.com sells birth supplies as kits.

Once a woman goes into labor, do not introduce anything in the birth canal; do not "check the progress" of her cervix or search for the baby's head. In an environment less than sterile and without IV antibiotics, infection can be introduced at this time that can prove deadly in a few days.

Allow her to squat or walk freely as this progresses the first phase of labor. Time her contractions and notice as frequency increases. When she begins to become irritable (okay, more irritable) or begins to say things such as "I can't do this anymore" she may be transitioning to delivery. There will be increased pressure on the rectal area as the baby's head moves into the birth canal. The caregiver needs to wash up with soap and water and put gloves on. Clean sheets need to be placed in the birth area— tucked up under the mother and over the lap of the caregiver so when the slippery baby comes out it lands in the sheet instead of on the floor. Babies are wet and become very cold very fast, so keep towels nearby to wipe the baby.

Each contraction will bring the baby's head out a little more. The baby's head will also go back a little on the resting side of the contraction—this is normal. The mother can push at this time as birth is imminent. The baby's head with be straight up or down. Once it has emerged, the baby will rotate to the side to clear the shoulders. Verify the cord is not wrapped around the neck. Remove the cord by gently slipping it over the baby's head. Gently help the top shoulder out of the birth canal with gentle pressure downward. The next contraction usually can push the other shoulder out. The rest of the baby will come out rapidly. Clean up the baby using the bulb syringe in the mouth and nose to clear airways. The baby can be gently stimulated by rubbing its back. Crying (the baby, not you) is a good way to get those airways clear. The cord can be clamped in two spots two inches apart and cut in between with sterile scapel or umbilical scissors. The placenta usually will deliver in a few minutes, so a bowl should be nearby to receive it. Do not pull on the cord. The whole placenta needs to come out as you will have to retrieve it if the cord breaks. The top of the uterus is now around the belly button and can be massaged once the placenta is out to reduce uterine bleeding. Massage until it is firm. This feels mildly uncomfortable to the mother. You may repeat as necessary during the twenty-four hours postpartum to reduce maternal bleeding.

The baby can be put to breast right away. Monitor both mother and baby for infection.

A Word About the Triad of Death and Severe Traumatic Wounds

Once medical data from the Afghan war became available, the term *traumatic triad of death* quickly emerged. This relatively new term describes three conditions and how they contribute to overall mortality in traumatic injury. The triad is hypothermia, acidosis, and coagulopathy. Hypothermia, a lowering of core body temperature, impairs enzymes critical to clotting processes. Hemorrhage compounds this by depleting clotting factors and reducing the body's ability to keep warm. Without red blood cells to carry oxygen and nutrients, cells lack the ability to burn glucose, causing lactic acidosis, and later on, metabolic acidosis. All of this further hampers cellular function and will eventually cause it to cease altogether. *Coagulopathy* is the medical term for either failure to clot or failure to clot properly, as is the case with disseminated intravascular coagulation (DIC), an advanced result of the triad, which is almost always deadly.

Staving off the hypothermic part of this triad does not require doctor's orders and by keeping the patient warm, dry, and covered you may save a life. If you have IV fluids, do not fluid overload—more than 2–3 liters will dilute circulation and drop platelet count, reducing ability to clot. Also, room temperature fluids will further cool the patient and hasten hypothermia, proverbially shooting oneself in the foot. This is a critical reason why I do not put too much stock in IV fluids. Most preppers I speak to at conferences want to have IV fluids in case someone gets shot or gets dehydrated from bad food or water. Noble, to be sure, but also well invested in the mentality of twenty-first century first world country wealth. I strive to have the statistical information necessary to stack the odds in the prepper's favor. It is far cheaper and less invasive to treat a dehydrated patient with the WHO rehydration solution than it is to purchase sterile fluids and sterile IV tubing and then get the training needed to start an IV in flat veins.

For the trauma from gunshot wound, again, look to the past. Statistics from the American Civil War show a full 50 percent mortality rate even with the medical training of the day. The reality is that only so much can be done if advanced medical care is not available. No one has the funding to turn their private residence into a sophisticated OR, complete with an off-grid power source for the ventilator, cardiac monitors, and lighting, or the storage area for all the equipment needed. A civilian prepper can store soap, clean water, and sterile medical supplies such as gauze to clean wounds. The perennial question for medical preppers is what to do with tourniquets if advanced medical care cannot be found within two hours of placing the tourniquet. Two hours is roughly how long a tourniquet can be in place without contributing to the injury, according to statistics available at this writing. I don't think there is an easy answer to this. You are not dealing with PVC pipe or engines requiring fuel. Human life is precious. If you choose not to store tourniquets or chest seals, the rapid hemorrhage from a gun wound will end the person's life quickly. If you do choose to stop the bleed and cannot get the individual to advanced medical care, you run a very real and high risk of severe infection from staph or gangrene from prolonged lack of blood flow to a limb. This is a horrible way to die. Personally, I have chosen to store and use tourniquets, QuickClot, and chest seals for gun wounds. All this morbid talk does lead me to one final topic before we move on: death.

Death

The subject of death is not exactly a way to start a conversation at a cocktail party. I have no desire to wax poetic here about it, but I do want to enlighten you with information I received from speaking with our county's coroner, Pat. Currently, the coroners' offices are chronically overworked and understaffed in South Carolina and most likely elsewhere. One would think with the American obsession with vampires and zombies there would be a line of qualified applicants waiting for the job. There is not. Death is dirty business. Our coroner processes between two to three people every day, 365 days a year. This is a small number,

TAKE SUCCESSIVE PICTURES
(GREEN LANE)

as our county has a population of approximately 120,000. However, she is the only staff member of the office. She has no assistants. She is hired full-time at forty hours per week. She actually works about sixty hours per week, paperwork being what it is. Can you imagine how easy it would be to overwhelm the system if there were a local catastrophic event? Of course other counties and states would pitch in. But in a large catastrophic event—such as a pandemic—what would she do? What could she do? She would be, as would other coroners, completely overwhelmed. So where does that leave the self-sufficient prepper? Again, as warned before, the judicial system may be down and out at the time of the catastrophe, but it will be working again, and when it does, you do not want to bring the wrath of the system down upon your head. How do you prove you didn't kill the person whose body you buried, thinking you were doing the right thing by preventing disease?

Here are Pat's tips: Keep a disposable camera in your Faraday cage or elsewhere to photograph your gravely ill patients. The coroner sees plenty of dead bodies—what they want to see is successive photographs documenting the decline and death of the victim. Keeping medical records with date and time is also extremely important in exonerating caregivers.

Once the person has passed away, the room needs to be sealed and the coroner called. (Really?) Yes, in the event of a disaster you will, at best, get a machine to leave a message. Leave the message with your address. If time passes and no police or other official has come to your house, you will be left with the unpleasant decision of what to do with a decomposing body. Pat suggests using an outside metal building as a temporary storage space for human bodies. It must be able to be locked and sealed to keep children and animals from entering. The body should be wrapped in sheets or garbage bags to contain body fluids as much as possible. All of this should be treated as contagious material and all involved should use gloves and masks. Photographs of the room where the person died should also be taken before the body is removed as police view this as a potential crime scene. ID of the person should be stored with their medical records.

Pat told me burial should not, from a legal point of view, be considered. If you must because of a pandemic, make the grave shallow and nowhere near water sources. The grave needs to be marked in some fashion so as not to appear as if you have something to hide. Do not burn the body, no matter how many medieval movies you have watched. This act is regarded by law enforcement as a deliberate method to conceal a crime, and you will be the one living to point fingers at.

Pat also pointed out she deals with approximately five suicides in an average week. This is during the good times of living in the prosperity of a wealthy first world country. It is naïve to think the whole neighborhood will be able to mentally hold it together when the world falls apart. Again, photography of the suicide scene and attempted contact with the coroner's office is the first thing to do. If officials do not arrive in a reasonable amount of time, the body will have to be moved to avoid it being subject to weather and wildlife. Witnesses can write an account of what they found and all papers can be put together with date and time on each and stored with the medical records. Any ID found can also be put with the records. If a weapon is involved, it is important that it be placed in a ziplock bag with recorded date and time and stored in a secure place to be given to authorities. I realize there are some people preparing for TEOTWAWKI who may be laughing at the idea of contacting overwhelmed authorities. Hopefully the case study below will illuminate the importance of following established laws.

CASE STUDY

A forty-nine-year-old surgeon practicing in an urban area goes to work the day a hurricane is predicted. The hurricane hits the hospital, where it causes shattering of windows. City power goes out, but generators kick in almost immediately, keeping life-saving equipment going. The surgeon carries on with the other hospital workers with minimal adjustments such as going without air-conditioning and lights. The next day, hospital workers are alarmed by water gushing from sewer grates in the street. Administrators decide to close the hospital and begin discussing what is going to be done about the fact that the emergency power transfer switches and generators are only a few feet above ground level. The hospital has no provision in its 246-page emergency documents for complete power failure or evacuation when streets are flooded. The surgeon, and the medical department chairman and other doctors meet in the afternoon and begin planning the evacuation of patients. Since they believe rescuers will be there in hours, they plan to evacuate babies first, then pregnant women and ICU patients. The patients with Do Not Resuscitate orders will go last.

The floodwaters rise and the building is plunged into darkness. The life-support systems will not operate without electricity. The National

HURRICANE DAMAGE IN NEW ORLEANS

Guard and private helicopters arrive by landing on the roof and begin to transport patients. Approximately sixty of the two hundred patients are removed by the second day. The hospital workers have now gone almost twenty-four hours with little or no sleep. The next day the building's temperature soars above 100 °F. Food and medicine supplies dwindle. There is more patient transport, but it is slow going and the state police will only stay until 5:00 p.m. Gunfire is heard outside and rescuers are shot at by malevolents. Few helicopters and rescue boats arrive as the emergency system is completely overwhelmed. The hospital workers hear the helicopters are being used to rescue people trapped on their roofs. Conditions continue to deteriorate as the hospital descends into hell. Nurses make their rounds with flashlights. Many cry as they cannot contact their loved ones. No one can leave as there are strict laws surrounding abandonment of patients. The staff has now gone forty-eight hours with only one or two hours of sleep. The toilets are backing up and the stench of raw sewage fills the halls.

The next sunrise is greeted with gunfire. Patients are given sips of water—virtually no IVs are being administered. The state has no resources to spare for movement of patients. Some patients in excess of three hundred pounds cannot be moved as there are no working elevators. The staff is exhausted. Some of the doctors, including our surgeon, run frantically between floors trying to calm anxious patients. The staff is running out of batteries for their flashlights. The hospital is no longer functioning as a well-run business or even a shelter. Everyone inside is trying to survive. The staff has now gone seventy-two hours with two or three hours sleep. Evacuations are primarily done by airboats run by civilians. The dead are moved to the chapel. The temperature inside the hospital is over 100 °F. One doctor abandons the hospital to try to rescue his son, trapped for three days on a roof. He was subsequently not charged with abandonment. By the fifth day the last living patient is removed from the hospital. The last of the staff is moved to a National Guard medical site. The exhausted workers will later tell the attorney general there were no IVs and no medicine left to care for the sick. The bodies will remain at the hospital in excess of ten days at 100 °F or more. There is simply no manpower to spare in the disaster.

DISCUSSION

This is the true story of Dr. Anna Pou, who was a surgeon in New Orleans and was at work the day of August 29, 2005, when Hurricane Katrina hit New Orleans. Her story, certainly traumatic, does not end here. Eleven months after the hurricane hit, Dr. Pou was arrested and charged with four counts of second-degree murder. Dr. Pou has dedicated her being to saving life. The attorney general, Charles Foti, felt there was evidence supporting the charges, based on autopsy results of morphine and midazolam in the victims' bodies. Approximately forty-five bodies were removed from New Orleans hospitals in the two weeks following Katrina. Approximately fourteen hundred people died in Hurricane Katrina.

In March of 2007 a grand jury was sworn in to consider Anna Pou's fate. The two nurses who assisted the good doctor were compelled to testify after the DA decided not to prosecute them. They both supported Dr. Pou. The general public was outraged by the doctor's arrest. Speakers at rallies to support Dr. Pou asserted that medical professionals would flee Louisiana in droves if a doctor was indicted after serving in a disaster. Ten counts were brought before the grand jury. She was not indicted on any of them.

In a brief interview after the decision, Attorney General Charles Foti stated he was "deeply regretful" the local grand jury had made their decision. He then added he felt as many as nine people were murdered in the New Orleans hospital.

Dr. Pou has since gone before the Louisiana legislature arguing for laws to shield health workers from civil and criminal liability in disasters. The state of Louisiana has agreed to pay retribution for her legal fees, which exceed $450,000. [source: *The New York Times,* "The Deadly Choices at Memorial" by Sheri Fink, August 25, 2009.]

Until laws are clearly written to protect health-care workers during the extraordinary stresses of catastrophes, preppers must always be cautious about "easing suffering" of patients. The above case concerns a physician, the most qualified person to make any decisions and diagnosis in any condition. The fact that the attorney general was ready to throw a surgeon, who is completely legally qualified to make all the decisions she made, into prison for the rest of her life clearly demonstrates the degree of aggressiveness that would be shown against lesser-trained persons. I must say that in light of this case I do not support stockpiling narcotics or other drugs that could be construed as euthanasia agents. Notice that this surgeon did not attempt surgery in this grid-down situation. She was simply administering the medications she had available as she judged best. Please always remember that law and order will eventually be restored and when that happens, documentation can both save and condemn you, but lack of documentation will more likely condemn you.

HEALTH AND FITNESS

Getting your body to work properly for eighty or so years requires some work and maintenance. Nutrition is important. Regular exercise is important. You don't know when you will be called upon to outrun the next zombie horde—just joking, of course—but the idea of being the last person in a stampede to escape death . . . isn't attractive. I remember seeing the scenes on television on September 11, 2001, of the crowds running away from the giant cloud of ash at street level in Manhattan and seeing some overcome by it. Almost three hundred people died at street level that day. In Aton Edwards's book, *Preparedness Now! An Emergency Survival Guide,* he mentions the privilege he had of being at Ground Zero twenty hours after the Towers fell. He remarked that among the chunks of concrete and shattered glass, he saw lots and lots of . . . high heel shoes. Apparently all the training in the world does a person no good if they try to run in four-inch heels. So here are some commonsense tips for your current lifestyle that will help give you the edge in a critical situation.

I am not going to espouse one diet over another. I do want to encourage you to consider the following ideas that will help you decrease your weight and increase your nutrition. They are in no particular order.

Health and Wellness Recommendations

- Take a multivitamin every day.
- Do not drink carbonated drinks, regardless of calorie content.
- Do drink clean water at least sixty-four ounces per day.
- Commit to sleeping at least eight hours per day.
- Brush your teeth everyday with a soft toothbrush.
- Address with a health-care practitioner any low-grade infections your body may be carrying, such as nail fungus.
- Wash hands with soap several times per day, after using toilet, and before eating.
- Eat like a king for breakfast, a prince for lunch, and a pauper for dinner.
- Use olive oil to cook with for its excellent essential fatty acid profile.
- Try to eat whole raw fruits and fresh vegetables every day; try to eat a greens-based salad every day.
- Consider taking magnesium supplements daily.
- Try to get in some form of exercise a few times a week.
- Try to laugh as much as possible every single day.
- Count your blessings of friends, family, and work every day.

EVERYDAY LIFE RECOMMENDATIONS

- Always keep your gas tank at least half full, and keep a water bottle and emergency blanket in the car.

- Always keep low heel shoes you can run in at your desk at work and in your car. It is even better if you wear them all the time, but this is not always possible.

- Consider carrying a small strobe LED flashlight in your purse or pocket. It can be used to disorient an attacker; it is vastly cheaper than a weapon and carries no legal restraints.

FITNESS

When it comes to fitness, we consulted with a good friend. Josh Harrison is a CrossFit Level 1 certified coach. According to Mr. Harrison, "fitness is absolutely critical for people who call themselves preppers. Time, money, and energy are spent preparing a homestead. Food and water resources are prepared. Alternative forms of energy are prepared. Maybe even protection through arms and ammunition is prepared. With all of this preparation, why would someone not want to prepare the number one resource that they have, their own body?" The only way to improve one's own physical preparedness is through some type of fitness regimen along with good nutrition.

Nutrition is the base of the pyramid of fitness, but please do not use the food pyramid that has been published for years. If you eat 6–11 servings of grain/pasta every day, you are heading toward health problems. Eat

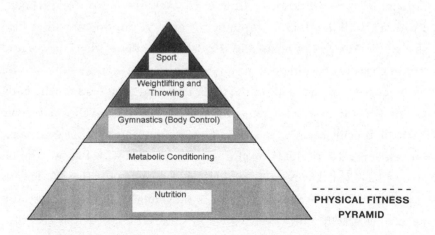

PHYSICAL FITNESS PYRAMID

NERD ALERT

WORK = FORCE X **DISTANCE.** You and I can both do the same amount of work if we both drag a sled loaded with 100 pounds of rocks for 100 yards. When we change the time domain, it gets interesting.

POWER = WORK/TIME. If you decrease the amount of time that it takes to complete the task, the power output increases. So, if I take half as long to drag the sled, I have actually doubled the output of power. This act of moving a large load over a long distance quickly (power) has amazing effects on the felt intensity in the body. It also produces the results that you want.

---

meats that are mostly lean. Eat fruits and vegetables. Also, add some nuts and berries. If you eat grains or pasta, keep the portions small. Stay away from highly processed foods. Eat as naturally as possible to increase health, longevity, and performance. This may have to change in a grid-down scenario. You may be eating stored foods that are not as healthy or natural. Health care may be scarce, so make the best of your resources now to prevent health problems when there is no available help.

Your fitness program should include many different types of functional exercises completed in a variety of combinations and time domains. There are a lot of functional exercises useful for preppers. Running, walking, hiking, climbing, or even swimming are all critical skills. These skills can be used in the daily activities of checking around the homestead, bugging out, or emergency rescues. These skills should be practiced with no load on the body first, and with load on the body as you become more fit. Grab your bug-out bag and take a small hike. You will quickly see why this training is so important. Other gymnastic movements such as squats, push-ups, pull-ups, jumps, or burpees should also be included. Any person should be able to maneuver their body with ease and strength. The last category of movements is weightlifting. You need to be able to move external weights. Movements such as deadlifts, squats, presses, sled drags, or even the Olympic lifts are great applications of force on an external object. They have wonderful carryover to working on a homestead or bugging out. All of these functional exercises should be combined and incorporated at various levels of weight, reps, and rounds. Time constraints must be used as well. Sometimes you will want to set a total time for the day's workout. Try to complete as many reps, or rounds, as possible within that limited time domain. Keep these between five and thirty minutes. At other times you will want to set the rounds and reps, but start a clock. Try to complete the workout as quickly as possible. The time component is what will make this work so well.

If you can afford equipment, it is an investment in your future. If you cannot afford equipment, be creative with what you have around the homestead. Lift heavy objects or packs. Make your own pull-up station. Keep variety in the program. Routine is the enemy. Your body must be prepared for anything. Always record your results and achievements for later reference. If you do repeat a workout that is timed, this will give you the ability to track progress. Don't ever forget recovery as well. Just do not spend more time recovering than you do working! A great resource that includes detailed explanations, varied exercises, and nutritional tips can be found on the Practical Preppers Mobile App by clicking on the Bug-out Work-out button.

BUG-OUT PLAN
When You Have to Leave!

There are a host of both man-made and natural emergencies that would prompt the need to evacuate. The short-term and long-term disasters include: nuclear events, wildfires (home fires, too), chemical spills, and hurricanes. The elderly and those who refuse to evacuate are at the highest risk of dying. In these situations, preplanned meeting sites are essential as you can waste hours trying to track down your child or spouse. If you are elderly, you need to prearrange transportation with family, friends, or neighbors. You may not have a working cell phone. Several years ago in our small town of three thousand, a tornado touched down at the elementary school. All the power went out in the town, and a trip across town that normally took twelve minutes became an arduous drive of seventy minutes. My wife was at the pharmacy, two hundred feet from where the tornado touched

TORNADO DAMAGE (ANDRZEJ19)

down, and I was driving from the school with our children. I came home to seven oak trees lying across a crushed and leaking roof. It took another hour before my wife could get home. The phone lines were down and we had only our premade plans to reunite. She could have wasted a lot of extra time and emotional energy had we not already made plans.

NUCLEAR DISASTER EVACUATION

During a nuclear emergency, a plan devised to evacuate the area by plant officials and local authorities will be enacted. If your child goes to a public school within the radius of the plant, you will not likely be able to reach your child at the school. The children will be transported to a preplanned site outside of the danger radius. If you live near a nuclear power plant, you should obtain a copy of the evacuation procedure and review it frequently with your family. A copy of the plan is often available at the local post office. Make your plans with your spouse, parent, or other responsible adult now: You will have one shot to execute it right.

NUCLEAR SYMBOL

If you are a pet owner, after reading the evacuation plan is a good time to talk about moving Fluffy. Make sure you have a pet carrier and leash. Make sure your pet has ID should it become separated from you. Your pet needs its own bug-out bag with food bowls, seventy-two hours of food, water, and diapers or kitty litter or other method to dispose of waste. Red Cross and most other shelters do *not* allow pets. You may want to find out if any hotels along your evacuation route take pets. If you have large animals, FEMA suggests they have identification and evacuate if possible. If relocating the livestock is not possible, decide whether to shelter them or turn them outside.

Whatever you decide, plan before the panic, and do not place the health of the pet before the well-being and safety of your family members. Time is of the essence if you want to beat thousands of other people evacuating. The roads will be congested and gas stations will be impossible to get in or out of as many people chronically run their vehicles below a quarter of a tank. As mentioned earlier, keep your vehicle's fuel tank at least halfway full at all times.

WILDFIRE

Wildfires come up so fast most folks simply run/drive for their lives with nothing more than the clothes on their back. To protect your home ahead of time, I encourage you to consider:

- Creating a safety zone with no combustibles within thirty feet of any structure.
- Install spark arrestors in chimneys and stovepipes.
- Use fire-resistant siding and roofing material.
- Either preburn or clear all debris within one hundred feet of any structure.

RAGING WILDFIRE

I encourage those who live in areas prone to fire to keep a bag in their cars that includes up-to-date bank statements, copies of Social Security cards, passports, birth certificates, recent photos of all family members, and all those other papers deemed irreplaceable. Some tech-savvy people keep that information on thumb drives.

URBAN FIRE EXAMPLE

My wife and I still remember the day in high school (we were classmates then) in New Lebanon, New York, where a fuel tank ruptured at a gas station a quarter mile away. The entire school population was rushed out into the parking lot and walked a half mile to the local park in the opposite direction. The entire evacuation was complete in less than one hour, to the credit of school and local officials. By the time our freaked-out parents found out, we were out of harm's way. It is a good example of proper municipal planning done in advance of an event.

CHEMICAL SPILLS

Chemical spills can literally render a town's water supply useless in a few hours. Chemical spills can occur from transport accidents—truck or train. Store water! Evacuation is usually necessary as some spills contaminate the air—one of the few scenarios where gas masks can save your life. West Virginia had a chemical spill in a major waterway in January 2014 that affected three hundred thousand people. For an entire week folks in nine counties and visitors to the capital city of Charleston were not only without clean drinking water, but their health was placed at risk if they merely inhaled the spilled chemical for an extended period of time.

FEMA mobilized approximately twenty-four hours after the disaster and donations of pallets of water poured in from neighboring states. An entire day is a long time for humans, pets, and livestock to go without

HAZMAT SUITS (JAREK TUSZYNSKI)

water, even during the wintertime. Imagine the enhanced level of panic if the Elk River chemical spill had occurred during the heat of the summer. The emergency is a good reminder why we need to have stored water at all times.

HURRICANES

The East and Gulf Coasts of the United States are prone to hurricanes. This area contains approximately one third of the U.S. population. Given the amazing intensity of these new superstorms, we hope that everyone has heightened awareness to weather on a daily basis. Hurricane preparedness at coastal level is intense as people must try to protect their homes with plywood, duct tape, tarps, and so on to safeguard their investment, and still get out of Dodge in a timely manner. Keeping bug-out bags in a coastal home is wise. The evacuation routes will clog quickly.

HURRICANE DAMAGE

HOME EVACUATION CHECKLIST

- Gather family; stay together.

- Unplug electrical equipment—coffeepot, radio, television. Keep refrigerators and freezers plugged in unless flooding is expected. (Exception: If advised by local officials to turn off all utilities, switch off all individual electrical circuits before shutting off main circuit breaker.)

- Shut off main water valve and natural gas/propane to your home.

- Secure windows and doors and cover windows with plywood or shutters.

- Bring in all outdoor furniture and items not tied down.

- Put bug-out bags in car. Take one car if possible to avoid separation.

- Leave a note in a conspicuous place detailing where you plan to go and how you can be reached. Some preppers disagree with this as it is an operational security breech. You will need to decide, given the situation, if you want to do this.

CACHES

There are many places to lay up some supplies on your evacuation routes. Some of our friends have gone so far as to dig holes in a farmer's pasture to sink a 5-gallon pailful of supplies. We recommend you not place yourself in a position of trespassing whenever possible. Also, as time goes by, landmarks may be cut down and the cache location will become indistinguishable.

We also recommend caching items on your own property. Bugging out can be as close as a cache location on your property. This could be a predetermined rendezvous point where everyone is to meet if the shelter is compromised in any way. The cache would provide a variety of survival items from food to firearms, from clothing to water filters. The techniques

PLASTIC SEPTIC TANKS MAKE GREAT CACHES!

for caching can vary greatly. We have used everything from ammo cans to buried plastic septic tanks (new ones) to 9,000-gallon fuel tanks.

Make sure your cache site locations are well documented and that you have various ways of finding them. Some people use GPS coordinates and their GPS device, others use a map and compass. We suggest using at least two methods; make sure you practice finding them. The failure to weatherproof your cache will come back to haunt you. Try to cache items where there is good drainage. Use containers that have a watertight seal. PVC pipe with glued-on end caps can be a great way to cache items. Vacuum

CACHES FOR KIDS

We have prepper friends with children in college. They have cached supplies at twenty-mile intervals with trusted friends. They place the map with markings in their student's bug-out bag. This gives the parents peace of mind that if their child had to walk home, a safe harbor would be within walking distance!

HOW TO GO GEOCACHING

Geocaching is fun process using a handheld GPS with its geocaching application to hide, find, and search for caches anywhere in the world. You will be amazed at how creative people can be at hiding things. The steps:

1. Search for nearby geocaches

2. Navigate to the geocache with the geocaching app or a GPS

3. Sign the logbook and log your find online

ASSORTED GEOCACHING CONTAINERS (CACHEMANIA)

seal items before you place them in a cache. You can actually vacuum seal larger items like rifles and then place them in PVC tubes. If you use PVC caches and you bury them vertically in the ground, make sure you are able to retrieve the items at the bottom. We take a small wooden disc that fits inside the PVC pipe with a hole in the middle of the disc that we thread a piece of paracord through, knot it, and then you have a way to pull all of the contents up and out of your cache without having to dig it up. Be creative and practice your caching!

BUG-OUT BAG ASSORTMENT

BUG-OUT BAGS (BOBS)

There are so many variations of bug-out bags. Get used to having one in your car and soon you will think of other things you want in it. If you live in an urban area and have frequent traffic jams, consider a way to address the call of nature! Some female preppers store diapers in their console.

Bug-out Bag: Basic List to Start

- Bag—backpack-style preferred
- Tarp or tent
- Small stove
- Sleeping bag or space-age blanket
- Pad for bag/blanket (to prevent hypothermia)
- Seventy-two hours of MREs or dehydrated food

EXAMPLE OF A WELL-BUILT BUG-OUT BAG

- Water filter or other purification method

- Insect repellant/sunscreen

- Fire starter

- Socks

- Small first aid kit

- Money (small bills)(on person)

- ID (this should be on person), documents

- Seventy-two hours medication

- Defensive weapon—pistol, knife, baton, pepper spray (note: weapons can be confiscated by Red Cross/National Guard if sheltering in a communal area)

- Paracord

- Hygiene (toiletries toothpaste, brush, etc.)

- Hatchet/shovel camp tool (this, too, can be confiscated)

- Maps or GPS; DeLorme makes topological maps

- A good quality compass

- Flashlight

- Radio—portable ham/ 2-way/NOAA Weather Radio

- Photos of immediate family (*Do not get separated!*)

- Night-vision goggles (if money is no object)

- Holy book

LEARN TO READ
A MAP AND
NAVIGATE

Strategies for the Bag

Where and how you anticipate traveling should determine your strategy for your bag. For example, I personally travel long distances to clients. I have a get-home bag. It contains things much different than, say, my wife's bug-out bag. I have several layers of defense in my get-home bag. I change the clothing in it to match the season. When your goal and motivation is to get home and take care of your loved ones versus bugging out to a cabin or a campsite in the woods for a couple of days, you will think differently about what is in your bag. Of course many items will be the same, but for instance, in my get-home bag I have a night-vision monocular. It allows me to travel at night and make great time as fewer people are on the roads. Now if I were bugging out with my family and we were on foot, it would be very hard for them to keep up at night and they could get easily hurt because they cannot see where they are walking.

Learn from Others

There is no exact science to how your bag should be supplied. You might be completely overlooking an item that could really help you. Our group decided to have a bug-out drill one week. A rendezvous point was chosen and an hour before the meet-up a text message was sent to everyone to "Bug Out!" When we all got together, we compared notes but also laid out the contents of our bug-out bags for everyone to see. We all took turns commenting on each person's bags. Some folks had so much gear that they couldn't carry it for more than a mile without seriously injuring themselves due to the weight. Others had items that were unnecessary or redundant. It was a fun and useful exercise that made me rethink and then reorganize our bags. I am fortunate to have access to the latest greatest preparedness equipment, so I do change out older items with the new and improved. I usually share these via a product review on my YouTube channel so others can know about them.

Possible Bug-out Bag Extras

- Rain gear
- Eyeglasses or contact lenses with solution, goggles
- Infant supplies—diapers, formula, bottles, pacifier, etc.

- Small child supplies—favorite toy/blanket, walking shoes (if child was scooped out of bed)

- Medium-sized bucket with lid and kitty litter (for bodily functions in the car)

- Season-appropriate extra clothing

- Signal flare—consider battery operated flares

- Small tool kit, crowbar, garbage bags

- Fire extinguisher, flame resistant poncho, smoke hoods

- Several bottles of water

BUG-OUT VEHICLES (BOVS)

This section is not about debating which bug-out vehicle is the best, but about what bug-out vehicle will work the best for your area, terrain, fuel access, and population density. The adage "Right tool for the job" certainly applies here.

For one group it might be the most tricked-out Ford F-550 Super Duty truck with every four-wheel drive accessory, camping gadget, and excess fuel capacity.

For another person it might be a folding bicycle with a rack that allows him/her to travel quickly out of a grid-locked city during an evacuation.

I want to share a few ideas with you and at least make you think about how you would "get out of Dodge."

For most people their daily driver will be their bug-out vehicle, so I don't want you to think you need to spend your lifesavings trying to outfit the ultimate BOV. If you have the resources or you think it would be a cool hobby to have then go for it, but I want you to be practical. Think about what form of transportation would give you the greatest chance of reaching your bug-out location or just getting to a safer place to shelter. When I am on the road and far from home, I think about what it would take to get home in the vehicle I am driving. I first think about fuel. That

is why I drive a diesel. I have tested many other fuels that I know will run in it other than diesel fuel, for example transmission fluid. This is getting harder to get away with on modern diesels, especially trucks, as they require you to have what is called diesel exhaust fluid (DEF) that is used to lower the NOx (nitrogen oxide) levels in the exhaust. The U.S. Environmental Protection Agency requires vehicle manufacturers to put measures in place to ensure that vehicles cannot run without DEF. If the truck is allowed to run out of DEF the engine's power is reduced, a solid red warning will be displayed, and the vehicle speed will be limited to five miles per hour until the DEF tank is refilled.

Can't You Drive?!

I was fortunate to grow up driving a variety of vehicles on farms and on terrains that they weren't necessarily designed for. From four-wheel drive vehicles to two-wheel drive cars and motorcycles, everything was tested in the woods, on snow, ice, and mud. You learn quickly what a vehicle can and cannot do by going off road. What I have learned and has surprised many people with me on trips through the woods is that a front-wheel drive car is remarkably versatile on most terrains. I say this to point out that if you have to get out of Dodge, and you have a front-wheel drive diesel car, you might be able to go places where the much larger 4x4 SUV cannot go. A front-wheel drive car in reverse will outclimb any two-wheel drive truck going forward. It is all about traction and weight distribution. Of course practice and knowing what your vehicle can do is important as well. Remember, the best BOV is the one that works for your situation, so don't be led astray by thinking you have to have a deuce and a half to escape NYC.

Here is a list of potential bug-out vehicles and their pros and cons:

AIRCRAFT

PROS—Cover great distances quickly, great for gathering intelligence

CONS—Cost, licensure, time in cockpit

SMALL AIRCRAFT

MILITARY TRUCK (GUY.COOPER)

MILITARY VEHICLES

PROS—Durable, huge carrying capacity, armored

CONS—Slow, poor fuel economy, highly visible

TRUCKS

PROS—Load carrying capacity, 4x4 off-road capability

CONS—Too large for urban maneuvering

SUVS

PROS—Increased passenger capacity, 4x4 capable, external carrying racks available

CONS—Too large for urban maneuvering

CARS

PROS—Fast and maneuverable, front-wheel drive preferred for traction, good fuel economy

CONS—Low ground clearance

BOATS

PROS—Access waterways, "road" less traveled

CONS—Slow

SAILBOAT

DUAL PURPOSE KLR650

MOTORCYCLES (DUAL PURPOSE)

PROS—Fast and highly maneuverable, reasonably priced, solution to gridlock, excellent fuel mileage

CONS—Limited passenger capacity, exposed to weather

ATVS

PROS—Can go anywhere, great load carrying capacity for size, safe and stable to drive

CONS—Not legal to drive on the road, tire noise can be heard for miles, exposed to weather

GOLF CARTS (GAS)

Pros—Relatively quiet, safe to drive, even children can drive

CONS—Expensive

OUTFITTED GOLF CART (LYNNGUEENY/LYNNGUEENY)

MOUNTAIN BIKES

PROS—Can go anywhere, can carry a lot of gear

CONS—Need a lot of them in good working order for a family

MOUNTAIN BIKE

SADDLED HORSE (THEWAKINGDRAGON)

HORSE

PROS—Can go anywhere

CONS—Have to be fed, housed, and properly cared for

BUG-OUT LOCATION

Most of what you will need at a bug-out location has been discussed in the shelter and power chapters. A few things to think about for a location where no one lives full-time are:

- Have enough fuel stored to make it there.
- Map out multiple routes.
- Stage supplies there.

- Install security equipment that can be remotely monitored.

- Have a separate cache or two of supplies at the location.

- Make it your vacation home so that you visit often, and the resources you would have spent on the "cruise" can go into a rewarding and sustainable lifestyle.

- If you have the resources, hire someone locally who can look after the place when you are not there.

SECURITY
Don't Be Caught Off Guard!

**Better to be despised for too anxious apprehensions,
than ruined by too confident security.**
—Edmund Burke

In the world we live in today, we see that the more dependent a society is, the more fragile it is when a crisis occurs. People get very demanding and violent when resources such as food, clean water, and electricity are not available. We believe that you should be prepared to protect yourself, your family, and your property. The majority of people whom I see preparing are concerned about an economic downturn, and they know from history that a bad economy leads to crime. This crime can begin as home invasions by a few individuals but can lead to organized marauders out to take whatever they want. We highly recommend that you develop a security plan. If you are one of those people who don't want to think about a security plan, we ask you to seriously reconsider your position. For those of you who only think about security please read the rest of the book and consider a more balanced approach to preparedness.

DEFENSIVE POSTURE PHILOSOPHY

The area where I have seen the widest variety of preppers is the field of security. One type is the "lone wolf" who depends on no one and plans on vanishing into the woods, eating jerky and edibles along the way. I do not think this is a viable solution as a single person can easily be severely injured—hypothermia from lack of shelter, trauma from rough terrain, and lack of medical care are just a few events that could occur in hours, not days. Another type is the military "warrior" who has served our country and has seen the horrors of war. I respect and honor each person's service and sacrifice to our country. The expendability of human life is the part I find to be a nonviable solution. I have seen several tactical strategies that are guaranteed to get someone killed. A family or small group does not have the support system of the army and no one in my family or group is expendable. Many folks are elderly or have physical limitations so they cannot run and gun with the twenty-year-olds.

It is illegal in every country in the world for civilians to kill each other, excepting in self-defense. If you do illegal things while TEOTWAWKI is going on, sooner or later the judicial system will be in working order, and the people who are legally allowed to expend life will be looking for you. You must, if you want to remain free, be able to prove you held a defensive posture. Defensive posture has many components. Working together to protect life and property is one part. Operational security, or OPSEC, is a military term that means keeping quiet about what you are doing, when, where, how, and with how many.

Making your house, your neighborhood, and your region as inconspicuous as possible to "bad guys" is your goal. Using OPSEC deprives the enemy of any information that might help him defeat you. The defensive term *situational awareness* refers to knowing what is going on around you. You need to have heightened awareness of the people around you to help you keep from being in the wrong place at the wrong time. To be able to do all this you will need to have short- and long-distance communication, lethal and nonlethal weapons, and multiple perimeter defense strategies.

COMMUNICATIONS:
THE LONG AND THE SHORT OF IT

A communication plan can be as simple as having a few handheld walkie-talkies (Handheld Transceivers [HTs]) or as complicated as having a ham shack with an extra class ham radio license and the renewable energy system to keep it running. Communication is the key to gathering information (intel) when a crisis occurs. If an EMP event occurred, the majority of people would not know what happened and there would be no standard broadcasts working to alert you. But having a radio would enable you to communicate with other members of your network, receiving and passing on early information that could be critical to your group's survival.

Short-distance communication

HTs greatly enhance your ability to defend or secure a location. If it is just you and your wife at your home, shelter, or bug-out location, being able to tell another person there is trouble brewing is so important. I use HTs on the jobsite when I need to communicate to a person on the other side of the property to tell me if the system we are working on is performing correctly. Radios save such a tremendous amount of time and have so many uses.

WOUXUN HT

I have recommended them to my customers as well for their everyday use as monitors for driveway alarms. When an object passes the sensor on a Dakota Alarm it sends an audible message to the radio. This is a great way to know when the FedEx truck is coming up the drive. If you practice with these things now, they can quickly be used to help you in a difficult time. Having a heads-up on whether or not someone turned into your driveway at 3:00 a.m. could mean the difference between life and death.

Ham Radio

Just saying it conjures up images of old men in a dark shed in the backyard who are part mad scientists and part electronics gurus. These "old guys" are able to talk to people around the world and even to the astronauts on the space station when it passes by.

Ham radio differs from MURS and FRS in that you need a license to be a ham radio operator. The license comes in three levels, technician, general, and extra. Getting into this potentially life-saving hobby has never been easier. I recommend you go to the site www.qrz.com to learn the language, take practice exams, and get an idea of what radio and antennas will work for you. I also recommend hooking up with someone who already knows what they are doing. Buy them a new battery for their ham shack and they will load more information on you than you can take in.

HAM RADIO STATION
(NATE STEINER)

In some regions of our country there are networks of like-minded folks who are able to reach out and touch someone without the use of repeaters. They have the power, the antennas, and the know-how to consistently receive and transmit messages to others. Some people have even set up their own repeaters to run off of sustainable energy if the grid goes down.

MURS

I recommend standardizing one type of radio for your shelter. For that radio, choose one with the longest range but at a decent price. There are so many types of radios but we recommend a dual band radio that can use the MURS frequencies as well as be programmed to work with most other types of radios. A dual band radio receives and transmits on both UHF and VHF frequencies. MURS has been the go-to system just as CB radios were in the past because it is an unlicensed service. Make sure you understand and follow the restrictions on wattage, antenna height, and where you are allowed to transmit and receive. RadioReference.com, eHam.net, and ARRL.org are three great resources for all things radio.

Most dual band radios will allow the operator to transmit on one band and receive on the other. Other arrangements include transmitting and receiving within the same band, but on two separate frequencies within that band. This is handy because if someone is listening to your conversation they are only going to get half of it. One additional but significant advantage to these radios is that they can also be used as a 2-meter ham radio.

The MURS radios we have been using are an integral part of our security gear. They come with all sorts of accessories like FBI-style ear mics, AA battery packs, specialized antennas, and cables for programming and cloning. The other great thing about MURS is that there are perimeter alerts that work on the MURS frequencies. So, if a vehicle comes up the driveway an alert is transmitted to the radio—and with that information decisions can be communicated about how to handle the situation. One little MURS HT radio can be used as a monitor, a short-distance communication tool, and a long-distance ham radio as long as you can open or connect with a local amateur radio tower. In my area I can open three different ham tower repeaters that technically allow me to transmit or receive a message all over the world. When it comes to the HT radios I also recommend having them in your vehicles. If cell service is interrupted, then you have a back-up communication system to call home. We have added magnetic mount antennas to our vehicles, and now we can communicate up to fourteen miles apart. Many preppers in our area have these so even if you can't reach home, you are likely to get ahold of a friend nearby who can lend you a helping hand.

Low-Tech Communications

Though they are not technically radios, field phones can be a great way to have local communication on your property, in your neighborhood, etc. They are not just for that rainy day event. Use them to communicate between buildings on your property. From the main house to the guest

FIELD PHONE
(ARNOLD REINHOLD)

house, from the barn to the RV or shelter, field phones can be used to call someone for supper! But in a crisis situation they really give you peace of mind in that no one can tap into your secure line. There are many varieties still available. Check with your local military surplus stores for availability.

Weapon Systems

Articles, forums, magazines, survivalists, and preppers keep the debates going: AK-47 versus AR-15; 1911 .45 ACP versus Glock. I have seen some beautiful collections of guns, knives, and assorted gear. I have also been disturbed by the people who have more weapons than food supplies. I am not against any certain amount or type of weapon, but if you don't have your water and food squared away then you or your group might be forced to turn marauder.

It has been said that a man with one gun who knows how to use it

AR-15 (JOE CEREGHINO)

AK-47

will be more valuable than the man who owns an arsenal but is unfamiliar with its contents. Those who teach tactical classes see this often. The students come to class with all their last-minute purchased gear, flagging others with their weapon and all around acting dangerously. You have to have patience to teach those classes.

I grew up using inexpensive standard caliber weapons: a Ruger 10/22, an H&R 20 gauge shotgun, a Winchester model 70 .30-06, and we always had an assortment of .22 pistols around and an occasional .357 revolver. I added a Winchester 1300 Defender 12 gauge to the list and so I had my basic set of weapons that could handle any type of game and defend my home. I still believe these are all great guns and are extremely useful for home defense and security. You can buy a 12 gauge shotgun a lot cheaper than a handgun these days.

I was introduced to my first SKS and AK about fifteen years ago and enjoyed shooting both of them. Both have a great reputation for dependability but not so much for accuracy. The more weapons that I was introduced to the more I realized the importance of standardizing equipment for a group of people working together to defend a location. Several retired military guys that I know all had multiple AR-15s and were extremely good at using them. Muscle memory is the key to being good with any weapon. Practice, practice, practice is what it takes to shoot well, have fast magazine changes, and minimize errors.

I decided that the AR-15 was the defensive battle rifle for me. At first, I was concerned about the small caliber, .233/5.56 grain, after being used to the 180 grain .30-06. But multiple thirty-round magazines make the difference when it comes to having fire superiority. I like the accuracy, the feel of it, and it's American made.

As for the "battle rifle" selection, you have just as many opinions when it comes to selecting a pistol. I will save the long lists and reviews for the experts like Sootch00 on YouTube. It usually boils down to two weapons in the pistol battle royal, the 1911 .45 ACP and the Glock. The Glock has a long track record of reliability but the 1911 is an American favorite.

KIMBER 1911 CUSTOM

GLOCK 17 (NUKES4TOTS)

Standardization of pistols for a group is important as well. If everyone has the same ammo and same magazines then everyone's weapons, parts, and ammo are interchangeable.

Tactical Training

Once you have chosen your rifle/pistol combination it is time for some tactical training. Training is typically broken down into two levels: Tactical Pistol and Close Quarter Marksmanship (CQM) with your rifle. You can also take precision rifle (sniper class) with a longer-range weapon like those in the .308 caliber category. Most trainers require a prerequisite class so that the student has his gear in order so he or she can get the most out of the class. Beyond that there are endless drills and tactics that can be learned from those who have had Uncle Sam's training courses. When you begin practicing with your group together is when you learn a whole new world of how to secure your location.

Load-Bearing Gear

When I went squirrel hunting as a young boy I put a box of loose .22lr (long rifle) ammo in my pocket and headed to the woods with the Ruger 10/22. I didn't have any fancy gear with all sorts of pockets and compartments. Today, the civilian world has access to the latest greatest gear, so you can be dressed from head to toe like those in the military. You can find

ESEE FIXED BLADE KNIFE

everything from helmets to ceramic trauma plates, to leg holsters and a ton of magazine pouches. Don't forget your knife. You should have a good heavy-duty fixed blade knife 4–6 inches in length. I recommend the ESEE brand but there are way too many good knives to choose from. Everything comes together on your tactical vest. Mag pouches, radio pouches, flashlight pistol holsters, and extra pistol mag pouches, medical kits, canteens, and CamelBak hydration packs can all be ergonomically arranged on your vest for ease of access. If you live in a big city and have tuned out because you can't have this tactical gear and lethal types of weapons, pay attention. You can still find ways to defend yourself that are highly effective. Tactical retractable batons, tomahawks, knives, pepper spray, bear spray, and a good old aluminum baseball bat are all highly effective tools to help you protect yourself and your loved ones. Just be sure to follow local laws on licensing and storing these weapons.

The Silent Shooters

Archery has its place among prepper weapons. First of all, nobody outlaws archery so no one is going to confiscate your compound bow. Secondly, bows are silent and therefore do not give away your location like

**COMPOUND BOW
(EWOK SLAYER)**

the blast of the deer rifle. Crossbows are fine for people who can't or won't become proficient with a bow. Slingshots have made a comeback and some people have modified them to be able to shoot arrows. A wrist rocket type slingshot can be used to kill any small game. When I was younger, I used a wrist rocket when I checked out traplines before school. I killed racoons, opossums, foxes, and muskrats without a problem.

Perimeter Defense Strategies

When it comes to security, if you do not have it in place 24/7 then you have no security. The mind-set of twenty-four-hour security is foreign to most folks living in a peaceful land. Those who are going to cause harm are going to be looking for weaknesses, so the further out you can deal with a

BARBED WIRE
FENCE

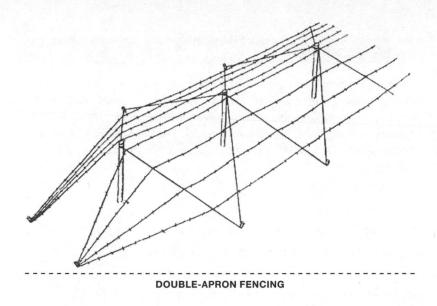

DOUBLE-APRON FENCING

potential threat the better. That is where an established perimeter comes in. First you need a perimeter to defend and nothing makes that more obvious than a fence. There are many styles of fence and some styles say "I am a loon" hunkered down for the apocalypse. Those who have an eight-foot chain-link fence with concertina wire on top and German shepherds patrolling the edges draw a little too much attention to themselves. We recommend using a fence that makes it obvious to both parties that if it is crossed it has to take some effort. Someone would have to cut, breach, or destroy the perimeter fence to end up on your property. I like fences you can see through. Welded wire or barbed wire fence used for livestock is a good starting point for perimeter defense. Later on, these fences can be further enhanced with techniques like turning it into a double-apron.

A double-apron fence really slows the intruder down, and all the while, you can see what they are doing. A stock of barbed wire is a must if you are going to build this defense. You can see from the illustration that this will take a lot of wire. A roll of barbed wire contains a quarter of a mile of wire so that will help you determine how many rolls you will need. If you don't want to get that elaborate, then consider using the same barbed wire to construct some *tanglefoot* on either side of the normal fence. Tanglefoot is simply creating a ground-level barrier that slows the intruder down. Of course, if you put up fence, then you have to have gates so you can get through. The gates are areas that need extra attention as they are typically easy to climb over or drive through.

Vehicle Stoppers

One technique for stopping a vehicle is to predig a drainage ditch in front of the gate, fill it with a culvert pipe, and then remove it when a time comes when you don't want people to be able to crash through your gate. Another method is to take premade barriers and block off the access. Militarily proven devices such as caltrops and hedgehogs can be fabricated ahead of time and used later on. Simply placing a log or dropping a tree across a road is an obvious deterrent. Since I raise cattle, I usually have about fifty round bales of hay that make great obstacles. Make sure you are doing this on your property.

Add as many force multipliers to your security plan as you can. Your security plan should work on the "onion theory," having as many layers as possible. The perimeter is the first layer but I will say if you can place alerts farther out down the street, the better off you will be. Alerts will give you time to gather your thoughts, gather your team, establish communication with everyone, and establish a plan of action. This is why I like Dakota Alerts because I can place them two miles from my shelter and determine if someone is coming down our street. Dakota Alerts use passive infrared

HEDGEHOG

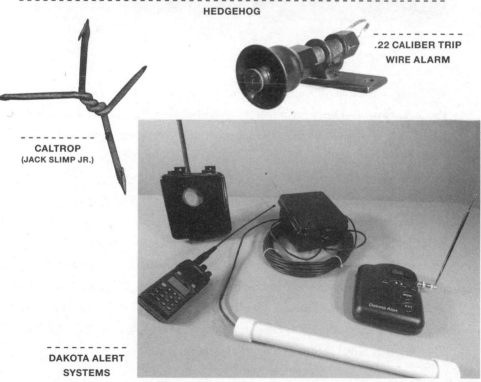

.22 CALIBER TRIP WIRE ALARM

**CALTROP
(JACK SLIMP JR.)**

**DAKOTA ALERT
SYSTEMS**

sensors that detect motion. For avenues of approach I recommend using the Dakota probe alerts as they sense anything metallic passing over them, whether it is a gate opening, a truck traveling, or a crossing ATV. I catch the UPS driver every day. He looks at me funny because I am always waiting on him when he gets to the house.

Other helpful devices are trip wires, trail cams, and infrared (IR) sensors. There are many trip wire and infrared sensors that are used in the wildlife management industry that will work amazingly well to help you detect two-legged intruders. There are alarms, strobes, and lights that can go off or you can use a silent radio transmitter method. You are only limited by your creativity. I really like the bear perimeter alarms as they can be run for great distances and the 12 volt system that powers them back at the shelter can be maintained by solar charging.

PERSONAL DRONE
(NICOLAS HALFTERMEYER)

Video cameras can also be used as we peel back another layer. Once the outer defenses are breached, then video cameras can be used for identification. Is it food (deer, rabbit, etc.) or is it foe? A lot of hunters today use some pretty sophisticated trail cameras that capture, record, and send images back to your cell phone or computer.

Drones

Small aerial drone technology keeps getting better and better. Imagine you are in your bug-out cabin and the perimeter alarm is sounded. Instead of putting you or anyone else in harm's way, you launch the drone and with its two video cameras you get to see in real time what or who set off the alarm.

Listening Posts/Observation Posts (LP/OPs)

Between your perimeter and your shelter you can place LP/OPs. Listening Posts/Observation Posts are usually concealed defensive structures that are positioned so that those on security detail can see as wide an area as possible with special emphasis on being able to see critical points of entry like gates or other important infrastructure. These LP/OPs can be part of an existing building or they can be purpose-built structures. They should not be easily seen by anyone. I like the #25 Pillbox design as this can be constructed quickly from corrugated culvert pipe and sand-bag barriers.

#25 PILLBOX STRUCTURE

The number of LP/OPs will be determined by the number of people you have to man them and the lay of the land so that fields of fire can overlap. The area of responsibility for one LP/OP should cross over with that of the LP/OP next to it, so that there are no gaps in your defenses. Though they can be positions to fight from, they are primarily early warning positions, so communication is essential from the LP/OP back to a communication center that would most likely be the command post.

Night Vision/FLIR

Of all the force multipliers available to the prepper today, I believe this is the most valuable, but of course it is also one of the most expensive items. The ability to operate at night as easily as in the day gives you so many advantages. Though you can mount the NVDs (Night Vision Devices) on your weapons I do not recommend it as is it very hard to maneuver in the dark while having to look down the barrel of your rifle. If you wear them,

Spot 32.4 °F

◆FLIR

43.6

-40.0

ε 1.00
Refl. t. 78
Obj. d. 3ft.

2013-02-02
5:07 PM

THERMAL IMAGING
(BLACK HILLS
THERMAL IMAGING)

PVS 14 NIGHT VISION

either on a helmet or a webbed holder, you are able to see normally. If you mount an infrared laser on your weapon then you have the best of both worlds. You can maneuver and shoot accurately. Forward looking infrared (FLIR) is another force multiplier that enables you to detect objects that emit heat. Warm bodies glow bright through a FLIR thermal imager. When you use FLIR and NVDs together you have the perfect system for the night. All three nighttime force multipliers can be found through JRH enterprises.

Self-Defense Training

We also recommend that you receive at minimum some basic self-defense training. There are so many martial arts practiced today that it might

ARE YOU READY TO DEFEND YOURSELF?

be hard to choose one. I recommend Krav Maga as it is simple, practical, instinctive, and aggressive. It also doesn't take you ten years of attaining belts before you have enough skills to defend yourself. The ability to block and strike, kick and submit can be learned in many ways, so try one. I took boxing for two years and tae kwon do for a year and the biggest thing I learned was to stay calm when you do get hit. Mike Tyson said, "Everyone has a plan until they get punched in the mouth"—so learning to cope with that feeling will give you a significant advantage in a combat situation. I also recommend you learn both gun and knife takeaway strategies. Getting self-defense training also can take care of your fitness training as well.

Security Disciplines

There are some security disciplines that most people do not think about, even those who are preparing. I have made videos on smell, light, smoke, and noise discipline, and people who have been prepping for a long time have thanked me for bringing at least one or more of these areas to their attention. If there is a crisis that results in any level of social chaos afterward we recommend that you stay put if possible and do not bring any attention to yourself or your location. Think about all the ways in which you can give away your location, especially if your preps are up and running. For example, the light shining from your apartment that you are running off of batteries charged by a Practical Preppers Crank a Watt Generator. If no one else has lights on, then yours are going to be obvious and will be seen for miles. Either douse the light or make sure you have an adequate way of blacking out your windows.

Smoke discipline comes into play for those who are running their woodstoves to stay warm and to cook their food. How do you stop the smoke? The number one factor in eliminating the smoke is to burn dry wood! Green, unseasoned, or wet wood gives off that white smoke that is mostly water. Another thing to think about is loading the fire early in the morning and late in the evening. The moisture of the wood will be burned off then and once the fire is going nice and hot, and the wood is dry, you will not see any smoke during the day. When it comes to keeping your shelter running, remember if your fancy generator is running all night, people will hear it from miles away. Make sure you put it in a building that is sound attenuated as much as possible. Check out the Engineer775 Practical Preppers YouTube channel and search for Discipline to find these and related videos.

Urban Security

If you live in the city, we recommend that you stay put during a crisis unless it is absolutely obvious or mandatory that you leave. Bugging out can land you in too many unknown and dangerous scenarios. Even if you cannot establish a nice neat perimeter with a radius of three hundred yards from your apartment you can employ many of the force multipliers mentioned above. Sensors, trip wires that set off an alarm or visual indicator, cameras,

URBAN ENVIRONMENT (CHRIS 73/WIKIMEDIA COMMONS)

NVDs can all be used to help you in a crisis situation. We also recommend you have material on hand to fortify your doors and windows. There are many great entry barricade systems on the market today.

Bunker/Safe Room

I am not a fan of the bunker approach to preparedness. I have heard people call their bunkers or safe rooms their "Alamo"! Don't they know that everybody died there? If you are totally outmanned and outgunned and you have to fall back to a last-resort position, I understand. However, do not take the Wild West method of defense where you knock out the windows and start shooting out of your home. Unless you have gone to

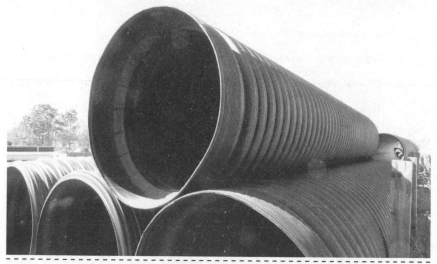

GREAT BUNKER/SAFE ROOM MATERIAL

great lengths to make it so your home is not a defensible structure. In
most cases if someone reaches your home, then you have lost the security
contest.

For regions that are prone to tornados and high winds we strongly
recommend a storm shelter. Even where I live, our family has gone into the
root cellar when the trees were coming down due to severe thunderstorms
and high wind shear. Obviously, an underground bunker is not the shelter
of choice if you live along the coast or any other flood-prone region. There
are many companies today that specialize in bunker building. Some start
with shipping containers and then reinforce them so they can be buried,
others start with large galvanized culvert pipes and then trick them out
from there. Others fabricate everything and build custom underground
bunkers for their clients. I am a fan of round-shaped anything when it
comes to burying stuff. Forces are equally distributed in round culverts or
large fuel tanks so the chance of anything caving in is minimized if, say, a
heavy vehicle parks on top of them.

Bunker Concerns

- Install two ways to exit.

- Have adequate ventilation for the number of potential occupants.

- Do not have heaters like woodstoves that emit carbon monoxide.

- Have fun things for the family to do to distract them from the event.

- Include the ability to communicate with the outside world.

- Use cameras or IR sensors to monitor what's going on topside.

PREPARING AND YOUR COMMUNITY

A Band of Brothers and Sisters

We must all hang together, or assuredly we shall all hang separately.

—Ben Franklin

The more prepared a community is, the safer it is. A neighbor's property and supplies are not potential targets in a crisis, when you are prepared. Prepared people can be part of the solution in a natural or man-made disaster. They can help others because their own needs have been taken care of in advance. Over the last few years I have let my neighbors know that I am preparing in hopes that they would also make preparations. I want them to know where I stand, not so they can come to me for help (though I do plan on helping to some extent), but so that they are not caught off guard by any crisis coming in the future. A prepared community is a resilient community. Sometimes the devastation is so overwhelming that you need help from others. A prepared community has the resources to help rebuild and a mind-set of looking out for one another.

Sheep, Wolves, and Sheepdogs

The "sheepdog" mentality is prevalent in the preparedness community. Most people are sheep, meaning they are kind, gentle, and peaceful and they depend on others to protect them. The wolves are the bad guys, the criminals who take advantage of the sheep. The sheepdogs of the community protect the perimeter and watch for wolves. Sheep find sheepdogs annoying when things are fine. I meet a lot of sheepdogs in the preparedness community and I believe it will take a lot of sheepdogs to defend their flocks if things get rough.

Networking

Networking is a term primarily applied to social media sites where knowing many individuals on a superficial level theoretically gives you an edge. I want to expand this idea to three levels:

- Regional networking
- Neighborhood networking
- Retreat networking

The regional network is connected by radio. Communication is the primary advantage to this group, although individuals within the group may network more closely. There may come a time where gathering information may become important—watching the movements of a vagrant band of miscreants as an example. This should be a discreet group. I encourage an organizer within the group to define bandwidths and times for broadcast. To belong to this group, members should have ham radio licenses.

A neighborhood network is already a known concept in our culture. There are signs in many suburban areas labeled "Neighborhood Watch." It means there is a group within that neighborhood who look out for each other's property and each other. You should establish some basic criteria in this group. The goal for the neighborhood is survival but it needs to be

WARNING

NEIGHBORHOOD WATCH

NEIGHBORHOOD WATCH

OUR NEIGHBORS ARE WATCHING
OVER ONE ANOTHER'S FAMILY MEMBERS AND
PROPERTY AND THEY HAVE BEEN TRAINED
TO REPORT SUSPICIOUS ACTIVITY
OR PERSONS IN THE NEIGHBORHOOD
TO OUR LAW ENFORCEMENT AGENCY

- - - - - - - - - - - - - -
COMMUNICATE WITH
THOSE AROUND YOU

discussed how that goal will be achieved. I hope where you live marauding is not considered an occupation. How much everyone is expected to share might also come up once everyone knows each other a little better. There will always be someone who does not want to take the time to participate, but will enjoy the full benefits of others' labor.

Basic Criteria for a Neighborhood Network

- Basic preparedness tenets require that each family maintains a certain degree of self-sufficiency so as not to be a burden to the rest.

- Each family needs to have at least one year's worth of food on hand for each of their family members.

- Each family needs to own at least one firearm. Many living in urban conditions fail to grasp the seriousness of being weaponless. If they choose to defend themselves with nonlethal means, it is their prerogative. To belong to the network, they need to own a firearm.

The most intimate level, the retreat network—that is, people you choose to shelter with, either on your property or theirs—will need more guidelines than the neighborhood. Rules and punishments will need to be clearly defined. We have been in a few agreements with folks through the years. If you reach a certain level of preparedness, almost always those who are less prepared will volunteer to come to your house. While some have suggested witty comebacks like, "Great! We can use fresh protein," it is more constructive to indicate you have some rules about who comes. Here are some of ours, learned mostly at the school of hard knocks.

- Like-mindedness. Common faith is central to community and governs decisions and behaviors. A basic preparedness philosophy is also necessary.

- Husband *and* wife need to be on board with prepping. This means both have a heart to learn more skills, are willing to work at manual labor, and put their resources into a well-rounded set of preps. What we have seen in the past is more like this: The husband has fifty guns, all with five thousand rounds of ammunition. The wife has her regular mani-pedi appointments at the salon, her designer purse with matching heels, and in general looks like a million bucks. She is *not* cleaning her own house now, much less making plans for an electrical disruption. Together they have four cans of beans, one bottle of ketchup, and a few diet sodas in the fridge. While he says he wants to come to your house when it gets bad, she is frantically trying to locate a restaurant on her iPhone. This is a situation to avoid at your retreat.

- The couple that has a skill set that you lack or are weak in. Perhaps he has former military service and can make decent recommendations and give some training to make you more defense oriented. Perhaps she has a degree and certificate in elementary education and you have small children. She could teach the children should school be closed for an extended period of time.

- A year's supply of food and other requirements. This is where the rubber will meet the road, if it didn't on the second point. Freeze-dried food is not sexy. It is not fun. It is not guns. It is a large expense, although one could argue since you can eat it, it is more an edible investment. It also takes great discipline to then open the cans and actually learn how to cook with them. And then replace them again. Yup, this one is where you lose all the people who think they want to come to your house. Also, if the retreat is on your property, you should require at least 50 percent of the food be staged there. Then you may add other requirements. Some I have heard are: five firearms with a thousand rounds each (preferably standardized with yours), antibiotics, sanitation supplies, cash, silver, etc.

- Don't ask anyone to be willing to do more than you do. If you do, it will create an uncomfortable hierarchy in people used to democracies. It is a fine line to walk, as you must also ask them to invest their time in your property before an event occurs, which makes it look like you are getting the better end of the deal. Some landowners will forgo this requirement and instead ask for an additional cash buy in beyond the above mentioned. This allows them to buy the additional infrastructure needed for people on the property. As a side note, we strongly discourage joint purchase of properties other than husband and wife. We have yet to see a happy ending in that situation.

- Government within the group. Few groups ever get to this level. It takes open and honest communication, as well as someone who understands the ins and outs of politics, such as a judge or Charles Krauthammer. Should people who are not blood relatives live together under great stress, it is usually only a matter of time before someone comes up (1) pregnant, (2) robbed, or (3) murdered. I spoke with a prepper recently who posed this question to me. Mind you, he has been part of a group for at least five years, and they are very advanced in their preps. He asked, how should widowhood be handled in a group? In our society, we have all sorts of ways to help single mothers and children. But if the group is the only safety net, how would a single woman do all the work of a couple traditionally led by a man? The answer is it would be impossible for her. The physical demands of primitive living would be too much without help—chopping wood, repairing machinery, planting, patrolling. So, a nice man in the group would need to do his own family work, and then hers. And how will he be repaid? What if he just declares her as his second "wife," not legally mind you, as the legal system is currently down for repairs. She cannot leave as it is too dangerous on the road, especially with children. You understand my drift. This is one example of fifty I could give you why you will need government in your group. A good start is an agreement to abide by the laws of the land (even if they are closed for repairs) and the reason why like-mindedness is the first requirement in a group.

Charity

Charity should come from the fountain of compassion within us. There are many people who have no such place inside, but those folks are not inclined to read a book like this. Currently we have several avenues in the United States to give of ourselves and our resources. Churches are a wonderful way to distribute your blessings in an anonymous way. I believe they will be an even better place as times get worse. Most churches now ask those who wish to receive charity to stay for a service and to be ministered to by the loving flock. Those who vehemently do not wish to hear of the Love of God leave. It is their prerogative. Most do stay, as their growling stomachs are reasonable and it is, after all, only an hour. The church we currently attend reaches out into our community to the impoverished with a huge food pantry and a separate church service. It is assumed they have access to clean water, although by the smell of some the elders may have assumed too much. In the future, water may indeed be a blessing. When you give charity you will want to remain anonymous.

BOTTLED WATER

CANNED FOOD

It may involve a separate trip to the church and meeting a deacon or elder to unlock doors while you bring in your donation. You will also want to make sure the deacon understands your desire for absolute anonymity— you do not ever want to hear that all the deacons know about your donation. You probably shouldn't ask for a receipt for tax purposes either. If you feel pretty paranoid about this point, and you should, since you do not want to attract requests for supplies you cannot spare, you may wish to locate a church well known for their outreach in another community and donate there.

If there is a total collapse and churches are no longer refuges, you will have to determine charity on a case-by-case basis. This will most likely involve your neighbors. They will figure out pretty quick you have more stuff than they do. They will expect decency from you—that is, the decency to feed their entire family, even though they went to Fun Park and you dry canned beans last summer. You have to get over this point. It is not fair, that is a fact. But that is not the point. The point is you have other humans that need, really need, to be fed, to have water, and to have their basic needs met. It will only make you bitter and hard if you remember they have great vacation pictures and you have calluses on your hands. If it angers you so much, go on vacation. Go, have fun. Don't resent them. You are being given a wonderful opportunity to truly impact their life for the better in a critical time. If they survive, they probably will never forget your generosity and love.

Go on, be brave. Make a difference while there is time for a difference to be made.

Barter Items

There are so many opinions about bartering. We are very fortunate where we live in that we have a local pasture that has been converted into a full-blown *jockey lot,* which is Southern for a flea market. There is a series of metal-covered pole barns—just old telephone poles with metal roofing. This is a trading extravaganza that occurs every Wednesday. Trading commences at sunrise, and you better get there early for the best deals. It is usually over by noon. Folks rent a table for $10 and sell. Literally, anything can be found there. There are vendors who drive between Florida and South Carolina carrying produce back and forth and are reliably there every week. Many have good reputations and sell produce at a fraction of supermarket prices. Dollars are the currency that is traded most right now, but I am sure this place will be hopping the day after the world as we know it ends. Bartering is a bit of an art, and I cannot say that I am really good at it. There is quite a bit of operational security to the art of bartering; you cannot reveal too much as you do not know the nature of the person you are dealing with. If it is a friend, you are simply trading. You trust them; they, you. No reason to be coy. However, in a prolonged catastrophe, which should be the only situation you barter in, you cannot be too sure of the other person's intentions.

Let me expound: There is charity for the poor person who has so little, or is so sick, that you, out of pity and compassion, feel moved to bless them, regardless of your own circumstances. In a perfect situation, the one receiving charity should show gratitude. They should not make any threatening moves or statements. Charity can never

> **ESTABLISHED BARTER ITEMS**
>
> Cigarettes ▪ Alcohol ▪ Chocolate ▪ Toilet paper ▪ Ammo ▪ Gold

be repaid, nor should you expect it. Charity has appropriateness to it; the person with no water bottle does not need a book; he needs a drink. You should not trade him his shoes for it.

Barter or trade has profit for both parties. One has a tangible asset the other wants. And it already gets tricky here. *How bad do they want it?* is the art of the barter. If one is too greedy, resentment will build. *Why do they want it?* I am inclined to give a can of formula to a man who claims to have an infant—I have no desire to squeeze every last asset he has out of him so he can feed his baby. Be very clear morally what you are seeking to profit from. Exploiting a situation will earn you a bad reputation. But you also need balance: If you give away too much you will be seen as the neighborhood resource and stripped of your assets. I have had the opportunity to e-mail with a person in the Philippines who was directly affected by Typhoon Haiyan. At his last mailing, he reported the neighbors were looking a bit jealously at all of his preparations. He was eating while they were not. He was drinking clean water while they were standing in lines. It really doesn't take the neighbors long to figure out something's up. He states his

CIGARETTES FOR TRADING
(GEIERUNITED)

neighbors had laughed at his preparations. I hope he is wise enough not to laugh at their lack of preparation. I hope he found the balance between charity and bartering.

The big question everyone asks is "What do I store to barter?" And I hear parroted at almost every conference: "Bullets—they will be as good as money when everyone is shooting every rabbit and squirrel in the woods." While it may be true that every animal's life expectancy will be shortened, it is *not* a good idea to trade bullets. You have no idea what the other guy plans to hunt. You do not know exactly how desperate is the person whom you are dealing with. And, worse, you do not know if he is figuring out how much resources you have so a group of his friends can come visit you at 3 a.m. armed and with lots of ammo.

We already have places that function for trade—these are pawn shops. Pawn shop owners are the masters of barter. According to Fernando Ferfal Aguirre, a survivor of the Argentinean economic collapse of 2001, these shops became the place to trade jewelry and other valuables into money as it inflated daily. I need to point out pawn shops tend to attract a crowd of wheelers and dealers who buy for next to nothing and sell extremely high. You may also notice the crowd's external appearances are "scruffy." It is not Macy's. You may want to check out your local pawn shops now and find out who is most reputable. You can do this by bringing a small item of known value into the shop and trading it. If you are ripped off

JUNK SILVER FOR BARTERING

now, you surely will be later. Notice the "local color" in the shop. If they are very interested in your trade with the shop owner, they know far too much about his business and can be gathering intelligence for reasons unknown to you (probably not good ones). So my first recommendation is to meet your local pawn shop owners. Sometimes jewelers will also buy "estate jewelry" and coins, so don't leave them out. You should make a few transactions so they get to know you. Notice what is being sold in the shop. This is already an indication of what the more impoverished in your area are already selling. If the shop cannot resell it, the market for it may be saturated.

One universal truth I have seen about American pawn shops is they all sell precious metal jewelry, precious stones, coinage, and weaponry. Another truth is you will spend lots of money on a piece of jewelry in a high-end jewelry shop, and you will get a little below scrap value for it at a pawn shop. The only way you make any money is if you inherit decent gold jewelry, and you can bet in real dollars (before inflation) it is still a loss. Barter items are hardly investment items. Barter items are what you sell because you need cash. It may simply be better for you to start storing cash. You will still need to pay utility bills unless you are off the grid. You will still need to pay the taxes on any property you own. You will still need to dress decently, especially if you have lost your job in the downsized economy and need to interview. Cash may ultimately become toilet paper, but you will still be able to spend it up until that day.

PREPAREDNESS CHECKLIST AND THE PREPPER REPORT CARD

PREPAREDNESS CHECKLIST

What are you prepping for? (e.g., economic, EMP, natural disaster, etc.)

YOUR LOCATION

State _____

Urban _____ Suburban _____ Rural _____

House _____ Apartment _____ Condo _____

How much land:

Lot _____ Acreage (How many acres?) _____

Size of group or family:

Adults _____ Teenagers _____ Children _____

WATER

What is your primary water source?

Municipal water _____ Well _____ Spring _____ Rainwater collection system _____

Alternative water sources in close proximity of house or retreat location

Check the ones that you could be using:

SOURCE	DISTANCE FROM YOUR HOUSE OR RETREAT
Lake	
Stream	
Pond	
Spring	
Others (list)	

What do you have to purify/disinfect alternative water sources?

_____

How many gallons of water can you treat and with what method?

_____

If the grid goes down how will you get your water to your home
(what method/pump)?

_____

How many gallons of water do you have stored presently?

_____

FOOD

How much food do you have per person in months based on 2,200 calories
per day if you could not resupply your group?

_____

What do you have to augment your stored food for your group?

SOURCE	NUMBER OR SIZE (SQUARE FEET)
Orchard	
Garden	
Greenhouse	
Aquaponics	
Rabbits	
Chickens	
Cows	
Goats	
Sheep	
Others	

Do you have heirloom or nonhybrid seeds put away and how much of each?

_____

_____

_____

FOOD PRESERVATION METHODS AND EQUIPMENT

Canning _____

Dehydration _____

Freezing _____

Root cellar _____

Smokehouse _____

NBC PROTECTION (NUCLEAR, BIOLOGICAL, CHEMICAL)

List the amount you have:

Protective masks _____

Protective suits _____

Radiation detection devices _____

Biological detection devices _____

Chemical detection devices _____

ALTERNATIVE HEATING PLAN FOR YOUR HOUSE

Woodstove   How much wood do you have stored? _____

Propane heater   How much propane do you have stored? _____

Other sources of heat _____

_____

COMMUNICATION PLAN (not counting cell phones or landlines)

Ham radio

CB radio

FMRS or GMRS

Field phones

ALTERNATIVE COOKING PLAN

METHOD	AMOUNT OF FUEL STORED (GALLONS, BAGS)
Wood cookstove	
Propane or Coleman fuel cookstove	
Charcoal stove	
Solar oven	
Other cooking devises	

ALTERNATIVE ENERGY

Back-up generator   Watt output

Solar system   Watt output

Other power system   Watt output

FUEL STORAGE PLAN

Diesel   Stored gallons

Gas   Stored gallons

Other

BARTER ITEMS

List items you are stocking as a alternative form of commerce, e.g., gold, silver, ammunition, common household items.

List _____

_____

_____

_____

MEDICAL SUPPLIES

Do you have a basic first aid kit?

_____

Other than the basic first aid kit do you have anything else medically that would be vital to have in an emergency where you are the only medical provider?

List _____

_____

_____

_____

Are you on any life-sustaining medications?

_____

_____

_____

FITNESS LEVEL

Are you at an acceptable fitness level to handle the stresses of a crisis situation?

_____

If not, what are you doing to prepare physically?
(e.g., CrossFit, P90X, running, etc.)

_____

_____

_____

_____

EVACUATION PLAN

Do you have a bug-out location (BoL)?

_____

How far from home base?

_____

Do you have a bug-out vehicle?

_____

Explain what makes it a bug-out vehicle.

_____

_____

_____

_____

_____

_____

Is your BoL stocked?

_____

Is it occupied?

_____

Is it kept secure?

_____

NETWORKING

Do you have a group of people you can count on?

_____

SITUATION AWARENESS OR RULES OF ENGAGEMENT

How will you handle situations when people come to you and your location for charity or to do harm?

_____

_____

_____

_____

_____

_____

_____

SECURITY

Have you done anything to enhance your security at your home or retreat to make it more easy to protect and defend?

_____

_____

_____

_____

Do you have the necessary items to provide for your own protection when there is no outside help?

ITEMS	AMOUNT
Firearms	
Ammunition	
Bullet resistance vests	
Night Vision Devices	

What other nonlethal weapons do you own?

_____

_____

What level of firearms or tactical training have you received?

_____

_____

_____

Do you have a library of self-help or how-to manuals that will help you deal with an emergency situation?

Do you have any special training or experience that you think would help you in an emergency?

_____

_____

_____

_____

_____

MILITARY TRAINING

Were you ever in any of the armed services? _____

What branch of service? _____

How long in the service? _____

What was your military occupational skill while serving?

_____

_____

_____

_____

_____

_____

Any other skill set beneficial to prepping? (e.g., electrician, plumber, seamstress, doctor, etc.)

_____

_____

_____

_____

_____

_____

PREPPER REPORT CARD

FOOD (20 POINTS)

10   Stored food (based on a year per person)

5   Food resupply plan (garden, orchard, livestock, fish)

5   Methods to preserve, resupply plan

WATER (20 POINTS)

10   Water already stored (based on 1 gallon per person for ninety days)

5   Water resupply (river, pond, lake, spring, well)

5   Method to purify, resupply plan

SHELTER (20 POINTS)

4   Location including bug-out location

2   Bunker/safe room

3   Power generation/fuel stored (solar, hydro, wind, generator)

3   Heating/cooling

3   Cooking

3   Medical

2   Barter Items

SECURITY (20 POINTS)

4   Training/experience (military, law enforcement, personal protection training)

4   Firearms and security enhancements (night vision, body armor, NBC protection, fortification)

4   Network/survival group

4   Communication

4   Bug-out vehicle

BUILD FACTOR (AKA X FACTOR) (20 POINTS)

5   Creativity

5   Engineering

5   Practicality

5   Effectiveness

ASSESSMENT

To determine how long you could initially survive a catastrophe, Practical Preppers has scored your preps in five categories of 20 points each, for a total possible score of 100.

FOOD: _____ OUT OF 20 POINTS

FOOD: _____ OUT OF 20 POINTS

SHELTER: _____ OUT OF 20 POINTS

SECURITY: _____ OUT OF 20 POINTS

BUILD FACTOR: _____ OUT OF 20 POINTS

Overall, you get _____ out of 100.

You have _____ months initial survival time.

SURVIVAL TIME IS BASED ON SCORE:

90–100   24 months

80–89   16–20 months

70–79   12–16 months

60–69   8–12 months

50–59   4–8 months

INDEX